OXFORD

W0232559

the grammar handbook

GORDON WINCH

OXFORD
UNIVERSITY PRESS

Oxford University Press is a department of the University of Oxford.
It furthers the University's objective of excellence in research, scholarship,
and education by publishing worldwide. Oxford is a registered trademark
of Oxford University Press in the UK and in certain other countries.

Published in Australia by
Oxford University Press
Level 8, 737 Bourke Street, Docklands, Victoria 3008, Australia

National Library of Australia Cataloguing-in-Publication entry

Author: Winch, Gordon, 1930– author.
Title: The grammar handbook/Gordon Winch.
Edition: Revised edition

ISBN: 9780195529098 (paperback)
Notes: Includes index.
Subjects: English language—Grammar—Handbooks, manuals, etc.
         English language—Usage—Handbooks, manuals, etc.
         English language—Punctuation—Handbooks, manuals, etc.

Dewey Number: 420

Text design by Sarah Hazell
Typeset by diacriTech, India
Indexed by Julie King
Printed and bound in Australia by Ligare Book Printers Pty Ltd

 c o n t e n t s

ntroduction

The *Grammar Handbook* is a guide to assist students with the essential rules of grammar, punctuation and usage of the English Language. It contains sections on all levels of traditional grammar and covers different text types. It is the perfect reference for students to dip in and out of when writing essays, presentations, etc.

To the student

This book is about grammar, which tells you how language works. You will be able to use it to learn the meanings of terms like noun, verb, conjunction, preposition and clause; how words are used correctly; how different types of speech and writing are put together; and how our language is used for different purposes.

I hope you will find it one of your most useful books.

Word level: the parts of speech

Nouns

> A noun is the name of a person, place, thing or idea.

Australia is a noun.   **Fun** is a noun.

There are many kinds of nouns. The four main ones are: *common nouns*, *proper nouns*, *abstract nouns* and *collective nouns*.

Common noun

A common noun is the name of any ordinary thing you can see and touch.

Here are some examples of common nouns:

dog	hat	ball
water	apple	car

The toy **dog** is made of metal.
Common noun

Proper noun

A proper noun is the special name of a person, place or thing. Proper nouns start with capital letters.

Here are some examples of proper nouns:

Mia	Canberra	Sydney Opera House
Captain Cook	China	

The **Sydney Opera House** is big.
Proper noun

Collective nouns

A collective noun is the name given to a group of persons or things.

Here are some examples of collective nouns:

team	herd	swarm
litter	bunch	flock

A **litter** of puppies.
Collective noun

Other types of nouns

Abstract nouns

An abstract noun is the name of something you feel, or something that could exist in your mind. You cannot see or touch an abstract noun.

Here are some examples of abstract nouns:

hope	sadness	joy	truth
love	kindness	greed	idea

Concrete nouns

A concrete noun is a noun that you can see or touch, like tree, hat or nose. It is the opposite of an abstract noun.

Here are some examples of concrete nouns:

floor	man	hill
ocean	ball	head

A concrete noun is a type of common noun.

Technical nouns

A technical noun is a noun that is used in a specific area of study. We only tend to use technical nouns when we are speaking or writing about particular topics.

Here are some examples of technical nouns:

fraction	oxygen	galaxy	triceratops

Non-technical nouns are also called *everyday nouns*.

A bear is a large **mammal**.
Technical noun

Terms-of-address nouns

A term-of-address noun is a noun we use when we are talking or writing to someone. It is a special type of proper noun.

Here are some examples of terms-of-address nouns:

Mrs Chin	Alex	Your Honour	Sir

Count or countable nouns

A count or countable noun is a noun that can be counted, such as *apple, leg* or *dog*.

We saw three **dolphins**.

I like **apples**.

Mass or non-countable nouns

A mass or non-countable noun is a noun that cannot be counted, such as fun, traffic or homework. For example:

You might say: The teacher gave us **more homework**. ✓

But you would never say: The teacher gave me ~~three homeworks~~. ✗

What heavy **traffic**!
Mass or non-countable noun

Verbal nouns (Gerunds)

Sometimes, a word can have more than one 'job'. A verbal noun, or gerund, is a verb ending in *-ing* that is used as a noun. In other words, it is an action word that is used to name something. (See Verbs, pp. 17–29.)

> **REMEMBER**
>
> A verb is a doing, being or having word!

Running is good exercise.	In this sentence, **running** is a verbal noun. It looks like the verb *to run*, but acts like a noun. It is the subject of the verb *is*.
I like **eating**.	In this sentence, **eating** is a verbal noun. It looks like the verb *to eat*, but acts like a noun. It is the object of the verb *like*.

I am good at **dancing**.	In this sentence, **dancing** is a verbal noun. It looks like the verb *to dance*, but acts like a noun. It is the object of the preposition *at*.
I went on a **walking** tour.	In this sentence, **walking** is a participle. It acts as an adjective, describing the noun *tour*.

Modal nouns

A modal noun shows a degree of possibility, certainty or obligation. That is, something that is possible, certain, or that you should do.

Here are some examples of modal nouns:

probability   certainty   necessity   chance

Compound nouns

A compound noun is made up of two or more words. These words may be joined together, as in *teabag* or *snowman*; or hyphenated, as in *self-control* or *brother-in-law*.

These are compound nouns:

bookshelf	thumbnail	goldfish
knife-edge	half-brother	sister-in-law

Sometimes when a group of words has a special meaning, we call them compound nouns, even though they are not joined together and do not have a hyphen. *Baked beans* and *human being* are compound nouns.

Noun group

A noun group is a word or a number of words based around a noun. It can consist of a single noun, a single pronoun, or a single noun with words built around the noun. A noun group can also include a clause. (See Groups, p. 38, Clauses, p. 42.)

In the following sentences, the noun groups are highlighted:

> **REMEMBER**
>
> A pronoun is a word that takes the place of a noun. Pronouns include words like **he, she, I, me, you, they, them**.

Dogs bark.

They bark.

Those dogs bark.

Those big dogs bark.

Those big dogs that live next door bark.

Noun groups are sometimes called *nominal groups* or *noun phrases*.

Noun phrase

A noun phrase is a phrase that does the work of a noun. (See Phrases, p. 38.)

These are noun phrases:

eating apples

going fishing

playing tennis

Playing tennis is fun!
Noun phrase

Noun clause

A noun clause is a subordinate clause that does the work of a noun. It can be either the subject or the object of a verb. A noun clause contains a subject and a verb of its own, but does not make sense by itself. (See Clauses, p. 42, Finite verbs, p. 20, Subject and object, p. 6.)

REMEMBER

A principal clause is a group of words that makes sense on its own. A subordinate clause is a group of words that gives meaning to the main clause of a sentence, but it cannot stand on its own.

What I saw at the movies was scary.	In this sentence, **What I saw at the movies** is a noun clause. It contains a subject (**I**) and a verb (**saw**), but it does not make sense on its own.
You must see **the game that is on TV tonight**.	In this sentence, **the game that is on TV tonight** is a noun clause. It contains a subject (**the game**) and a verb (**is**), but it does not make sense on its own.

More about nouns

Person

Nouns and pronouns have person. There are three types of person:
first person, *second person* and *third person*.

- **First person** refers to the person who is speaking: *I*, *me*, *mine*, etc.
- **Second person** refers to the person who is being spoken to: *You*, *yours*, etc.
- **Third person** refers to the person being spoken about: *he*, *she*, *it*, *mum*, *dad*, *Tom*, etc.

The superhero is flying.
Third person

All nouns are in the third person. They are always 'spoken about'. (See More about Pronouns, p. 11.)

Number

A noun has number. It can be *singular* or *plural*. Singular means one. Plural means more than one.

apple **singular**   apples **plural**

Forming the plural

In English spelling, the plural is formed in different ways. Always use your dictionary to check, if you are not sure.

Many singular nouns add **-s** to make the plural:

boy → boys   girl → girls   toy → toys

Others add *-es*:

beach → beaches   fox → foxes   church → churches

If a noun ends in *y* and has a consonant before the *y*, the plural drops *-y* and adds *-ies*:

baby → babies   lady → ladies   ruby → rubies

Nouns ending in -*f* or -*fe* make the plural in two ways.

- They add -*s*:

  chief → chiefs   roof → roofs

- They change -*f* to -*v* and add -*es*:

  knife → knives   loaf → loaves

In some cases, both plural forms are acceptable:

handkerchief → handkerchiefs → handkerchieves

hoof → hoofs → hooves

Nouns ending in -*o* form the plural in two ways.

- They add -*s*:

  piano → pianos   merino → merinos

- They add -*es*:

  potato → potatoes   tomato → tomatoes

Compound nouns form the plural in two ways.

- They add -*s* to the end of the compound:

  spoonful → spoonfuls

- They add -*s* to the first part of the compound.

  sister-in-law → sisters-in-law

Some singular nouns that come from foreign words
change their endings altogether:

crisis → crises   plateau → plateaux

Some singular nouns change their vowels to form the plural:

woman → women   man → men

Sometimes they change their consonants as well:

mouse → mice   louse → lice

Some singular nouns do not change to form the plural at all:

deer → deer   sheep → sheep

Gender

Nouns can be *masculine* (male) or *feminine* (female).

Some nouns are neither masculine nor feminine. These are called *neuter*. Masculine,
feminine and neuter are a noun's gender.

Some nouns can be either masculine *or* feminine. These nouns are said to be *common gender*.

EXAMPLES OF NOUNS AND THEIR GENDER			
Masculine	Feminine	Common gender	Neuter
boy	girl	child	rock
man	woman	human	tree
father	mother	parent	drink

Nominalisation

Nominalisation is the process of making nouns from other parts of speech. For example, the verb *lose* becomes *loss*; the adjective *high* becomes *height*; the verb *dwell* becomes *dwelling*.

Some words can be nouns or verbs, depending on what their job is in a sentence. For example, the word *jump* can mean 'a jump' (noun) or 'to jump' (verb).

I did a huge **jump** on a trampoline.   I like **to jump** on a trampoline.
Noun   Verb

Case

Nouns and pronouns have case. Case refers to the relationship between nouns (or pronouns) and verbs. (See Pronouns, below.)

There are three main cases:

- The *subjective case* refers to the subject of a verb. The subjective case is sometimes called the *nominative case*.
- The *objective case* refers to the object of a verb or preposition.
  The objective case is sometimes called the *accusative case*.
- The *possessive case* shows ownership of something.

Ahmed borrowed Stephen's book.   In this sentence, **Ahmed** is in the subjective case. It is the subject of the verb *borrowed*. **Book** is in the objective case. It is the object of the verb *borrowed*. **Stephen's** is in the possessive case. It tells us who owns the book.

> **REMEMBER**
>
> The subject is the person or thing who performs the action of the verb.
> The object is the person or thing who has the action of the verb done to them.

How do we find the case of a noun?

Subjective case	Ask **who** or **what** in front of the verb. **Who** *borrowed the book?* *Answer: Ahmed*
Objective case	Ask **who** or **what** after the verb. *Borrowed* **what**? *Answer: the book*
Possessive case	Ask **whose**. **Whose** *book was it?* *Answer: Stephen's*

Pronouns

A pronoun is a word that is used instead of a noun.

Maria is my friend.
She will be having a birthday party on Saturday.   In the first sentence, Maria is a noun. In the second sentence, the word **she** is used instead of Maria. **She** is a pronoun.

There are many different types of pronouns.

	Pronoun	Type of pronoun
She is having a party.	she	personal pronoun
It is quite simple.	it	personal pronoun
The book is **mine**.	mine	possessive pronoun
I knew the boy **who** was hurt.	who	relative pronoun
That is my dog.	that	demonstrative pronoun
What is the time?	what	interrogative pronoun
He hit **himself** with the bat.	himself	reflexive pronoun
The Captain, **herself**, spoke.	herself	emphatic pronoun
Anyone can play.	anyone	indefinite pronoun
Each of us has a bike.	each	distributive pronoun

Personal pronouns

Personal pronouns are used instead of the nouns that name people, places, things and ideas.

Like the nouns they represent, personal pronouns may be the *subject* or *part of the subject* of a clause or sentence. They can also be the *object* or *part of the object* of a clause or sentence.

Personal pronouns have a lot in common with nouns:

* They have case—*subjective, objective* or *possessive.*
* They can be singular or plural.
* They have person—*first person, second person* or *third person.*

Personal pronouns: subjective case

The personal pronouns in the subjective case are the *subjects* of a clause.
The subjective case is also called the *nominative case.*

He found the book. In this sentence **he** is a personal pronoun and is the subject of the verb **found**. As the subject, it is **subjective case**.

> REMEMBER
>
> To find the subjective case, find the subject! Ask *who* or *what* in front of the verb.

The personal pronouns in the subjective case are:

	First person	Second person	Third person
Singular	I	you	he, she, it
Plural	we	you	they

The pronoun *you* can be singular or plural!

Personal pronouns: objective case

The personal pronouns in the objective case are the *objects* of a clause.

He found the book and gave **it** to **her**. **It** is a personal pronoun and is the object of the verb *give.* As the object, it is objective case. **Her** is a personal pronoun and is governed by the preposition *to.* Because of the preposition, it is objective case.

The personal pronouns in the objective case are:

	First person	Second person	Third person
Singular	me	you	him, her, it
Plural	us	you	them

REMEMBER

To find the objective case, find the object! Ask *who* or *what* after the verb.

The cats were sleeping.
The dog saw **them**.
Personal pronoun, objective case, third person

A personal pronoun can be an indirect object. In some sentences, there is more than one object. There's the person or thing that has the action done to them, and there can also be another person or thing that can be affected by that action.

Ali gave **me** the book.

This sentence really means, *Ali gave the book to me*. So, the direct object is *book*, because it is the thing that has the action done to it. The indirect object—the person affected by the action—is **me**.

A personal pronoun can be the object of a preposition.
(See Prepositions, p. 33.)

The teacher gave the pencils to **her**.

In this sentence, the personal pronoun **her** is the object of the preposition *to*.

Personal pronouns: possessive case

The personal pronouns in the possessive case are:

	First person	Second person	Third person
Singular	mine	yours	his, hers, its
Plural	ours	yours	theirs

Personal pronouns in the possessive case are also called *possessive pronouns*.

REMEMBER

Possession tells us about ownership. To find the possessive case ask **whose**.

Possessive adjectives

There are some words that seem like pronouns, but are only used with nouns. They are called *possessive adjectives*. (See Possessive adjectives, p. 13.)

That dog is **mine**.
Personal pronoun, possessive case, first person.

This is **my** dog.
Possessive adjective

Relative pronouns

A relative pronoun is a pronoun that is used to link a subordinate clause to a noun or personal pronoun. This noun or pronoun is called an *antecedent*.

The relative pronoun has to agree with the antecedent in person and number. If the antecedent is first person, singular, the relative pronoun must also be first person, singular. If the antecedent is third person, plural, the relative pronoun must also be third person, plural.

David, **who** is eight years old, is playing in a band.	In this sentence, **who** is the relative pronoun and *David* is the antecedent. *David* is third person, singular, so **who** must also be third person, singular.

Here are some common relative pronouns:

who   whom   which   that

Who and whom

We use the relative pronouns *who* and *whom* when we refer to people.

- *Who* is used for the subjective (or nominative) case.

The girl **who** lives next door came over to play.	The relative pronoun **who** is in the subjective case because it is the subject of the verb *lives*.

- *Whom* is used for the objective case.

I like the team captain **whom** you chose.	The relative pronoun **whom** is in the objective case because it is the object of the verb *chose*.

- *Whom* is also used when it is the object of a preposition.

With **whom** did you play in the tennis match?	The relative pronoun **whom** is the objective case because it is the object of the preposition *with*.

When we speak, we often replace *whom* with *who*. Writing is usually more formal, however, so we should use *who* and *whom* correctly.

Which and that

We use the relative pronouns *which* and *that* when we refer to animals, places or things. But be careful—they don't always mean the same thing!

You can catch the train, **which** goes every ten minutes.
You can catch the train **that** goes in ten minutes.

In the sentences above, *which* and *that* both refer to the word *train,* which is the antecedent. But the sentences have different meanings. The first sentence refers to a train that goes every ten minutes. The second sentence refers to a particular train that goes in ten minutes' time. (Hurry or you'll miss it!)

Interrogative pronouns

An interrogative pronoun is a pronoun that is used to ask a question. Interrogative pronouns are sometimes called *question pronouns*.

The interrogative pronouns are:

who   whom   whose   which   what

If one of these words is followed by a noun, it becomes an *interrogative adjective* or a *pronominal adjective*.

> **REMEMBER**
>
> An adjective is a word that modifies or gives us information about a noun.

Which book is the best?
Interrogative adjective

Demonstrative pronouns

A demonstrative pronoun is a pronoun that refers to a specific noun. Demonstrative pronouns are often used when we can point to the people or things we are talking about.

The demonstrative pronouns are:

that   this   those   these

If one of these words is followed by a noun, it becomes a *demonstrative adjective* or a *pronominal adjective*.

Reflexive and emphatic pronouns

Reflexive and emphatic pronouns are made by adding *-self* (singular) and *-selves* (plural) to the end of a personal pronoun.

Reflexive pronouns are often used when the subject and object are the same. In other words, when a noun or pronoun does something *to itself*.

He hurt **himself.**	In this sentence, **himself** is a reflexive pronoun because it refers back to the *he* who is the subject of the sentence. The subject and object are the same person.

Emphatic pronouns are used to emphasise, or draw attention to, the noun. They are often used to demonstrate that something interesting or important has happened—or that it has been done by someone important!

The premier **herself** visited our school yesterday.	In this sentence, **herself** is an emphatic pronoun because it draws attention to the noun *premier*. It tells us that *the premier* is an important person.

Indefinite pronouns

Indefinite pronouns are pronouns that we use when we don't want to refer to any particular person, place or thing.

No one is to blame for this mess.

Indefinite pronouns that end with *-one* or *-body* refer to persons, while those ending in *-thing* refer to places or things.

Here are some examples of indefinite pronouns:

one	none	anyone	someone
no one	nobody	anything	nothing

Indefinite pronouns are usually followed by a singular verb.

Distributive pronouns

A distributive pronoun is a pronoun that refers to individual members of a group separately, rather than to the group as a whole.

Each had a carrot.
Distributive pronoun

The distributive pronouns are:

each   every   either   neither

If these words are followed by a noun, they become *distributive adjectives* or *pronominal adjectives*. (See Distributive adjectives, p. 14.)

Each lamb had its wool clipped.   **Distributive adjective**

More about pronouns

Person

A pronoun has different forms depending on its person. There are three persons: *first person, second person* and *third person*.

- **First person:** This refers to the person who is speaking.

  I am an athlete.

  We all run in the City to Surf.

  It is **mine**.

- **Second person:** This refers to the person being spoken to.

  You will be late, Tom.

  You will be late, children.

  You have won the prize, Jo. It is **yours**.

  You have won the prize, children. It is **yours**.

- **Third person:** This refers to the person being spoken about.

  I wouldn't trust **him**.

  Theirs are in the wash.

  I wouldn't trust **them**.

Number

Pronouns have number. Some are singular and some are plural.

If the noun it refers to (the *antecedent*) is singular, the pronoun is also singular. If the noun it refers to is plural, the pronoun is plural.

In the examples that follow, the nouns/antecedents are highlighted in bold, with an S for singular or a P for plural placed above each.

S I have a new **bike**. **It** is made of metal.	The noun **bike** is singular, so the pronoun **It** is also singular.
P The **kids** can't wait for the school term to end. **They** love holidays!	The noun **kids** is plural, so the pronoun **They** is also plural.

Here are some more examples:

Personal pronouns: **The footballers** trained hard. ➤ **They** trained hard.

Possessive pronouns: That is **John's**. ➤ That is **his**.

Demonstrative pronouns: **The answers** are correct. ➤ **These** are correct.

Gender

In English, there are four genders. They are:

* masculine (male)

* feminine (female)

* common gender (can be either male or female)

* neuter (neither male nor female) (See Gender, p. 5.)

Examples of pronouns and their gender

Masculine	Feminine	Common gender	Neuter
he	she	he or she	it
him	her	him or her	

Nouns have gender, and so do pronouns. A pronoun has the same gender as its *antecedent*, the noun it replaces.

In the examples that follow, the antecedent is in brackets following the pronoun. It has an M for masculine gender, F for feminine gender, N for neuter gender and C for common gender written above it.

F M **She** (a girl) sat next to **him** (a boy).	**She** is feminine and **him** is masculine.
N **It** (a building) will have to be demolished.	**It** is neuter.
M N **I** (Fred) have **nothing** (money) left to give.	**I** is masculine and **nothing** is neuter.
C **Anyone** (man and woman) who knows him C will join **us** (men and women) today.	**Anyone** and **us** are common gender.

Pronouns and the very special verb *to be*

The verb *to be* is special because it has its own rule relating to case and pronouns:

The verb *to be* takes the same case after it as before it.

This is because *to be* links a subject to a **complement**, which is something that is needed to complete the meaning. The verb *to be*, in its many forms, is sometimes called a **linking** or **relating verb**.

The rule means that the subjective case form of the pronoun is used before and after the verb.

It is she who was lost.　　It is the subject of the sentence and **she** is the complement. **Is** is part of the verb *to be*.

In the sentence above, you might expect that *her* would be correct, because *her* is the normal objective form of the pronoun. But *she* is correct because it is the complement of the verb *is*.

Here are some more examples:

It is they who need to pull up their socks.

It was she who did most of the work.

It is I who baked the cake.

> **REMEMBER**
>
> A complement is a word that is needed to give meaning. Prepositions such as *with* and *under*, and verbs such as *be* and *feel* need a complement to make sense: **with** *me*, **under** *it*, **be** *happy*, **feel** *hungry*.

This rule is gradually changing, because many people feel that it is very old-fashioned. However, it is still important in formal writing.

Adjectives

> An adjective is a describing word. It describes or adds meaning to a noun or pronoun.

In each of the following phrases, the adjective describes a noun:

a **tall** building   **Tall** is an adjective. It describes the noun *building*.

a **hungry** cat   **Hungry** is an adjective. It describes the noun *cat*.

In the following sentence, the adjective describes a pronoun:

She is **funny**.   **Funny** is an adjective. It describes the pronoun *she*.

(See Adjectival phrases, p. 39 and Adjectival clauses, p. 44.)

There are many types of adjectives. They all describe nouns or pronouns.

a **strong** boy

descriptive adjective

Descriptive or describing adjectives

These are the most common types of adjectives. *Big*, *small* and *happy* are descriptive adjectives. They tell us about the qualities of a person or thing. Descriptive adjectives can be divided into *factual adjectives* and *classifying adjectives*. Factual adjectives tell us about the qualities of a person or thing, as in *kind person* or *big ship*. Classifying adjectives place something into a group or type, as in *Siamese cat* or *Australian history*.

Possessive adjectives

A possessive adjective shows possession.

This is **my** bike.

Possessive adjective

Possessive adjectives have to match the person and number of the nouns and pronouns that they modify.

	Singular	Plural
First person	my	our
Second person	your	your
Third person	his, her, its	their

Possessive adjectives *must* be followed by a noun. Possessive adjectives are sometimes called *pronoun adjectives* or *pronominal adjectives*.

Numeral or numbering adjectives

A numeral adjective describes the number or numerical order of nouns or pronouns.

two geese
numeral adjective

There are two different kinds of numeral adjectives: *cardinal adjectives* and *ordinal adjectives*.

- Cardinal adjectives tell us the number of things: *ten* toes, *eleven* players, *one* cake, etc.
- Ordinal adjectives tell us the order of things in a numerical sequence: *first* runner, *third* song, *tenth* biscuit, etc.

Numerical adjectives are sometimes called *quantity adjectives*.

Demonstrative adjectives

A demonstrative adjective is an adjective that demonstrates or points out a specific noun.

In the following sentences, the demonstrative adjectives point out a noun:

This hat is mine.	**This** points out the noun *hat*.
That hat is yours.	**That** points out the noun *hat*.
These shoes are mine.	**These** points out the noun *shoes*.
Those shoes are yours.	**Those** points out the noun *shoes*.

Demonstrative adjectives are sometimes called *pointing adjectives* or *determiners*.

Distributive adjectives

A distributive adjective is an adjective that refers to individual members of a group separately, rather than to the group as a whole.

Each cat was howling.
Distributive adjective

The distributive adjectives are:

each   every   either   neither

Remember that distributive adjectives refer to individual things, so each is singular in number and requires a singular verb.

Neither Bill nor Jane **is** here.

Each bird **catches** a worm.

Interrogative adjectives

An interrogative adjective is an adjective that asks a question. In the following sentences, the interrogative adjectives are highlighted:

Which animal made that sound?

What make of plane is that?

Whose friend is waiting?

Interrogative adjective or interrogative pronoun?

In some sentences, the question words **which**, **what** and **whose** are used as interrogative adjectives. In other sentences, they are used as interrogative pronouns.

How can we tell the difference?

If the question word is followed by a noun, it is an interrogative adjective:

Which horse finished last?

If the question word is not followed by a noun, it is an interrogative pronoun:

Which finished last?

Modal adjectives

A modal adjective shows an amount of probability or certainty.

> a **possible** event
>
> a **definite** result

Words like **certain**, **likely**, **unlikely** and **probable** are modal adjectives.

Indefinite adjectives

Indefinite adjectives refer to number but do not give the exact number.

Some, *few*, *many* and *most* are examples of indefinite adjectives in the following sentences, because each modifies a noun:

> **Some** people are very kind.
>
> **Few** parents would come to the show.
>
> **Many** children are swimming.
>
> **Most** cars are shiny.

When an indefinite adjective is not followed by a noun, it is called an *indefinite pronoun*. (See Indefinite pronouns, p. 10.)

More about adjectives

Adjectives and degree

Most adjectives show degree. Degree is used to compare things. It tells how much more or less.

There are three degrees: *positive*, *comparative* and *superlative*.

- Positive is the first degree. It describes a particular quality of something: *My dog is* **strong**.
- Comparative is the second degree. It compares a particular quality of two things: *My dog is* **stronger** *than Rory's dog.*
- Superlative is the third, and highest, degree of comparison. It compares a particular quality of more than two things: *My dog is the* **strongest** *dog in the world!*

> **REMEMBER**
>
> There is no degree between the comparative and the superlative. We should never say that something is 'more bigger' or 'more stronger'!

Many adjectives take the endings *-er* for the comparative and *-est* for the superlative. Here are some examples:

Positive	Comparative	Superlative
big	bigg**er**	bigg**est**
soft	soft**er**	soft**est**
ugly	ugl**ier**	ugl**iest**
small	small**er**	small**est**

Sometimes, the spelling of the adjective changes when *-er* and *-est* are added. Always check your dictionary if you are unsure!

Some adjectives seem clumsy if you add *-er* or *-est*. They form their comparative and superlative forms with the adverbs *more* or *most* instead. Here are some examples:

Positive	Comparative	Superlative
beautiful	**more** beautiful	**most** beautiful
delicate	**more** delicate	**most** delicate
reliable	**more** reliable	**most** reliable
horrible	**more** horrible	**most** horrible

REMEMBER

The superlative is the highest degree of comparison. We should never say that something is 'the most biggest' or the 'most beautifullest'!

Some adjectives have irregular forms:

Positive	Comparative	Superlative
good	better	best
many	more	most
little	less	least
bad	worse	worst

Absolute words
Some adjectives do not have a comparative or superlative degree. They are sometimes called *absolute words*. For example, if something is **empty**, it cannot be more or less empty. (See Making sense, p. 121.)

Here are some absolute words:

    full   dead   correct   perfect   whole   equal

Fewer and less
The adjectives *fewer* and *less* are often confused, but they are used in different ways. (See Count/countable nouns, p. 2.)

* *Fewer* refers to numbers of things. It is used with *countable nouns*:

   Fewer people crossed the bridge.

* *Less* refers to quantities. It is used with *non-countable nouns*:

   Less butter is needed in the cake.

Fewer is always followed by a plural noun. This means that any verb that follows the noun will also be plural.

    Fewer apples were on the tree.   **Apples** is plural, so the verb *were* is also plural.

Less is followed by a singular noun:

    Less water was on the road.   **Water** is singular, so the verb *was* is also singular.

Verbal adjectives (participles)
A verbal adjective, or participle, is a verb ending in *-ing* that is used as an adjective. In other words, it is an action word that is used to describe a noun. (See Participles, p. 20; Gerunds, p. 2.)

A verb is a doing, being or having word!

He went on a **walking** tour.	In this sentence, the word **walking** is an adjective because it describes the noun *tour*. But it also acts as a verb because it refers to an action—something someone does.
He is **walking** down the street.	In this sentence, the word **walking** is part of the verb *is walking*. It is the present participle.
Walking is good exercise.	In this sentence, the word **walking** is a verbal noun. It is the subject of the verb *is*.

Here are some more examples of verbal adjectives:

a **falling** rock   a **swimming** lesson   a **performing** seal

Verbs

A verb is a doing, being or having word.

Here are some examples of verbs:

scratched   was   have

My cat **was** angry.
Verb

Verbs are different kinds of processes, that is, they are things that are going on. Verbs tell us what is happening.

There are many kinds of verbs. In the following sentences, the verbs are highlighted:

I **like** ice cream.

You **won't like** it.

My sister **walked** home.

Dad **should cook** tonight.

The movie **will be** good!

I **have read** that book.

Doing verbs

There are four different types of *doing* verbs: *action verbs*, *saying verbs*, *sensing verbs* and *relating verbs*.

The bird **flew**!
Verb

- Action verbs involve an action—something that is done.
  Run, jump and *flew* are action verbs.

- Saying verbs involve speech—something that is said.
  Shout, whisper and *scream* are saying verbs.

- Sensing verbs involve thought and feelings—something that is sensed or felt.
  Love, remember and *imagine* are sensing verbs.

- Relating verbs involves linking or relating—how pieces of information are linked.
  Be, have and *become* are relating verbs.

Action verbs

In the following poem, the action verbs are highlighted:

Me—Moving

I **dart** and **dash**,
I **jig** and **jump**,
I **scamper**,
skate and **scramble**.
I **strut** and **stride**,
I **slip** and **slide**,
And frequently I **amble**.

I **leap** and **lurch**,
I **crawl** and **creep**,
I **rove** and **romp**
and **ramble**.

I **turn** and **trip**,
I **skid** and **skip**,
And now and then—
I **gambol**.

Gordon Winch

Saying verbs

Here are some examples of saying verbs:

ask	demand	explain	agree	suggest
reply	shout	whisper	murmur	say

Sensing verbs

Here are some examples of sensing verbs:

Thinking	Feeling	Perceiving
reflect	love	know
recall	hate	notice
forget	like	observe
wonder	fear	see

Relating verbs

Some verbs do not show actions, thoughts or feelings. These verbs simply link pieces of information in the text. They tell us how one piece of information relates to another. That is why they are called *relating* or *linking verbs*.

Here are some examples of sensing verbs:

Being	am	is	mean
Having	has	possess	include

Other types of verbs

Auxiliary verbs

An auxiliary verb is a verb that 'helps' another verb or participle to make a complete verb. For example:

I **have read** all of my books!	In this sentence, **have** is the auxiliary verb and **read** is the verb that it helps.
I **am going** for a walk.	In this sentence, **am** is the auxiliary verb and **going** is the participle that it helps.

Auxiliary verbs are very important, because they make it possible for us to give a clear sense of time. We use auxiliary verbs to form the different tenses of verbs. (See Tense, pp. 24-6.)

Here are some examples:

Past tense:	I **was** hungry.
Present tense:	I **am** singing.
Future:	I **will** go to the shops tomorrow.

The main auxiliary verbs are *to be, to have, to do* and *will*:

to be:	am, are, is, was, were, been
to have:	have, has, had
to do:	do, does, did

The verb *will* has no other forms. It is always *will*.

> **REMEMBER**
>
> An auxiliary verb is a verb that is used with other verbs or participles to complete a verb. For example, 'I **have** seen that movie'. Auxiliary verbs are also called **helping verbs**.

Modal verbs

Modal verbs give us information about the amount of possibility or certainty being expressed. They are usually auxiliary verbs.

* Some modal verbs express low modality or certainty—things that **might** happen.
* Some modal verbs express medium modality or certainty— things that **can** or **should** happen.
* Other modal verbs express high modality or certainty— things that **will** or **must** happen.

Here are some examples of modal verbs:

Low modality	Medium modality	High modality
may	should	must
might	can	will
could	need to	have to

Modality

Modality can be expressed with other parts of speech, not just with verbs.

Modal nouns	Modal adjectives	Modal adverbs
possibility	possible	possibly
probability	probable	probably
necessity	necessary	necessarily

Negative forms of verbs

So far we have talked about verbs in the positive form, but we can also make verbs negative. We do this in two ways.

* If there is an auxiliary verb, we add the word **not**:

Positive form	Negative form
I **have** worked hard.	I **have not** worked hard.

- If there is no auxiliary verb, we add **do not** or **does not**:

Positive form	Negative form
I **play** football.	I **do not play** football.
He **plays** football.	He **does not play** football.

Negatives can also be *contracted*, or made shorter.

I **have not** worked hard. ➤ I **haven't** worked hard.

I **do not play** football. ➤ I **don't play** football.

He **does not play** football. ➤ He **doesn't play** football.

Finite verbs

Verbs can be *finite* or *non-finite*.

A finite verb has a subject, and can stand alone in a clause or sentence. It does not need another verb to make sense. Every clause or sentence must have a finite verb.

The tree **crashed** to the ground.	In this sentence, **crashed** is the finite verb and *the tree* is the subject.

To find the subject of a finite verb, you ask *Who?* or *What?* before the verb.

Question: *What crashed?*

Answer: *The tree.* So *tree* is the subject and *crashed* is a finite verb.

REMEMBER

A sentence must have a finite verb and a complete meaning!

Non-finite verbs

A non-finite verb cannot stand alone as the main verb in a sentence. It needs another verb to make sense. (See Sentences, p. 46, Clauses, p. 42.)

to see the movie	This phrase does not make sense. **To see** is not a finite verb. We need to add a subject and a finite verb to turn this phrase into a sentence.
We went to see the movie.	This is a complete sentence, because it has a subject and a finite verb.

There are two kinds of non-finite verbs: infinitives and participles.

Infinitives

The infinitive is the basic form of a verb. It has no subject, and is usually preceded by the word *to*.

Here are some examples:

to dance   to eat   to hear   to walk   to swim   to stay

An infinitive can appear without the word *to*:

I did not dare **ask**.	In this sentence, **ask** is in the infinitive form. It is a much less clumsy way of saying *I did not dare* **to ask.**

Participles

There are two kinds of participles: *present participles* and *past participles*.

Present participles

The present participle of a verb is made by adding the ending *-ing* to the infinitive. It combines with an auxiliary verb to make a complete verb.
(See Compound and Auxiliary Verbs, p. 18.)

I **am walking** on the footpath.

The complete verb is **am walking**. The auxiliary verb is **am** (a part of the verb *to be*) and the present participle is **walking**.

Infinitive	Present participle
(to) dance	danc**ing**
(to) move	mov**ing**
(to) stay	stay**ing**
(to) try	try**ing**
(to) walk	walk**ing**

Past participles

The past participle of a verb is usually made by adding the ending *-ed* to the infinitive. It combines with an auxiliary verb to make a complete verb.

I **had walked** on the footpath.

The complete verb is **had walked**. The auxiliary verb is **had** and the past participle is **walked**.

Infinitive	Past participle
(to) dance	danc**ed**
(to) move	mov**ed**
(to) stay	stay**ed**
(to) try	tri**ed**
(to) walk	walk**ed**

A number of irregular verbs form their past participles in different ways. Here are some examples:

Infinitive	Past participle
(to) be	been
(to) see	seen
(to) do	done
(to) drink	drunk
(to) fly	flown

We have **flown** over the mountain.
Irregular past participle

Transitive and intransitive verbs

A transitive verb has an object. The word *transitive* means *to pass over*. The action 'passes over' from the verb to the object.

The man **sailed** the yacht.

In this sentence, the action passes over from the verb, **sailed**, to the object, *yacht*.

To find out if a verb has an object, ask *Who?* or *What?* after the verb.

Question: *Sailed what?*

Answer: *The yacht.* So *yacht* is the object and *sailed* is a transitive verb.

An intransitive verb does not have an object.

> The rain **stopped.**   This sentence has no object, because the action does not pass over from the verb, **stopped,** to something else.

Question: *Stopped what?*

Answer: There is no answer, because there is no object.

So the verb *stopped* in this sentence is intransitive.

Agreement in person and number

Finite verbs are limited by, or tied to, the subject. They must agree with the subject in *person* and *number*.

Person

Pronouns have three persons:

First person:	**I** like ice cream.
Second person:	**You** like ice cream.
Third person:	**He** likes ice cream.

Nouns are always in the third person.

> **Ciara** likes ice cream.
>
> **Children** like ice cream.

Verbs must change in order to agree with the 'person' of the subject.

First person:	I **like** ice cream.
Second person:	You **like** ice cream.
Third person:	Ciara **likes** ice cream.

Irregular verbs, like the verb *to be*, have more changes.

First person:	I **am** on holidays.
Second person:	You **are** my friend.
Third person:	He **is** my brother.

(See Nouns pp. 1–6, Pronouns pp. 6–13, Agreement, p. 42.)

Number

Nouns and pronouns have number. They can be *singular* (one) or *plural* (more than one).

If the subject of a clause or sentence is singular, the verb must be singular.

If the subject is plural, the verb must be plural. That is, the verb must agree with the subject in number. (See Clauses, p. 42.)

Here are some examples:

> This horse jumps fences.

Singular subject	Singular verb	Object
This horse	jumps	fences.

These horses jump fences.

Plural subject	Plural verb	Object
These horses	jump	fences.

Singular or plural?

Sometimes, it can be difficult to work out whether the subject of a verb is singular or plural.

Here are some common situations that often cause confusion:

- When using words that end in -s but are singular:

  The news **is** good.

  Maths **is** easy for some people.

- When using words that look singular but are plural:

  The police **work** hard to protect the community.

  Cattle **are** herbivores.

- When using subjects with *and*:

  → The verb is plural if there are two persons or things:

  My sister and brother **are** good fun.

  → The verb is singular if the subject refers to one person or thing:

  Lemon and lime **is** my favourite flavour.

- When using *either ... or*; *neither ... nor*:

  → If both parts of the subject are singular, use a singular verb:

  Neither he nor I **is** going.

  She or I **is** playing.

  Either of my friends **is** invited.

  Neither of my parents **likes** rock music.

  → If one subject is singular and one is plural, the verb agrees with the nearer subject:

  Neither John nor they **are** going.

  Neither they nor John **is** going.

- When using a collective noun subject:

  Collective noun subjects, such as *team*, *class*, *herd* or *gang*, are singular or plural depending on the meaning of the sentence.

  The team **is** arriving today.   (The team as a whole—singular)

  The team **are** putting on their shorts.   (The team as individuals—plural)

- When using the subjunctive:

  If you are expressing something that you imagine might happen—that could happen, that might happen or that is just in your imagination—you must use the subjunctive mood of the verb:

  If I **were** there ...

  If he **were** on our team ...

Tricky?! Never mind, there aren't many of these cases!

The subjunctive mood requires you to change the usual rules of subject/verb agreement in terms of number (singular or plural) with subjects that are in the singular. You would usually say *I was...* or *He was...* (See Subjunctive mood, p. 26.)

More about verbs

Tense

Tense refers to time. It tells us when the process or action is taking place. There are three main tenses: the *past tense*, the *present tense* and the *future tense*.

- The past tense tells us that the action has already taken place:
  My mother **liked** school.
- The present tense tells us that the action is taking place now:
  I **like** school.
- The future tense tells us that the action will take place some time
  in the future:
  My baby sister **will like** school.

Each of these tenses has a number of different forms. These are:

- the simple form
- the continuous form
- the perfect form
- the perfect continuous form.

The simple form

The simple form consists of short forms of the present, past and future tenses.

Simple present tense:	I **walk** to the beach.
Simple past tense:	I **walked** to the beach.
Simple future tense:	I **will walk** to the beach.

The timeless present

The timeless present tense is another form of the present tense. It refers to actions that do not change. They keep going on, at the same time, always. They are part of the scheme of things.
Bears hibernate all winter.
Flowers bloom in the spring.
The timeless present looks like the simple present, but there is a difference. The simple present tense talks about things that are happening right now, and things that happen regularly.
'I **fly** really high.' (happening now)
I **have** an egg for breakfast every Sunday. (happens regularly)

The continuous form

The continuous form tells us that the action or process *is*, *was* or *will be continuing*. The continuous tenses use the verb *to be* with the present participle.

Present continuous tense:	I **am helping** my mum today.
Past continuous tense:	I **was helping** my mum last weekend.
Future continuous tense:	I **will be helping** my mum this weekend.

The perfect form

The perfect form tells us that the event, action or process *is complete, was completed* or *will be completed*. The perfect tenses use the verb *to have* with the past participle.

Present perfect tense: He **has helped** a lot of people.

Past perfect tense: He **had helped** a lot of people.

Future perfect tense   He **will have helped** a lot of people this year.

The perfect continuous form

The perfect continuous form combines the *perfect* and the *continuous* forms in the present, past and future tenses. It uses the verbs *to have* and *to be* with the present participle.

Present perfect continuous tense:	She **has been helping** many people.
Past perfect continuous tense:	She **had been helping** many people.
Future perfect continuous tense:	She **will have been helping** many people.

REMEMBER

The verb must agree with the subject in person and number!

TENSES

Simple	Continuous	Perfect	Perfect continuous
Present			
I jump	I am jumping	I have jumped	I have been jumping
You jump	You are jumping	You have jumped	You have been jumping
He/she/it jumps	He/she/it is jumping	He/she/it has jumped	He/she/it has been jumping
We jump	We are jumping	We have jumped	We have been jumping
You jump	You are jumping	You have jumped	You have been jumping
They jump	They are jumping	They have jumped	They have been jumping
Past			
I jumped	I was jumping	I had jumped	I had been jumping
You jumped	You were jumping	You had jumped	You had been jumping
He/she/it jumped	He/she/it was jumping	He/she/it had jumped	He/she/it had been jumping
We jumped	We were jumping	We had jumped	We had been jumping
You jumped	You were jumping	You had jumped	You had been jumping
They jumped	They were jumping	They had jumped	They had been jumping
Future			
I will jump	I will be jumping	I will have jumped	I will have been jumping
You will jump	You will be jumping	You will have jumped	You will have been jumping
He/she/it will jump	He/she/it will be jumping	He/she/it will have jumped	He/she/it will have been jumping
We will jump	We will be jumping	We will have jumped	We will have been jumping
You will jump	You will be jumping	You will have jumped	You will have been jumping
They will jump	They will be jumping	They will have jumped	They will have been jumping

> **Shall and will in common usage**
>
> Today, most people form the future tense by adding the verb *will* before the verb. Traditionally, people also used the verb **shall**.
>
> Shall and will were used in different situations:
>
> - **Shall** was used for the first person personal pronoun, singular and plural:
>   *I shall be helping.*
>   *We shall be helping.*
> - **Will** was used for the second and third person personal pronouns, singular and plural:
>   *He will go shopping on Saturday.*
>   *They will go to the beach on Sunday.*
>
> To show emphasis, however, **will** was used for the first person and **shall** for the second and third person:
>   *I will win this race.*
>   *They shall be caught.*
>
> Nowadays, most writers don't make this distinction, and **shall** is seldom used.

Mood

Mood refers to the way the process or action is expressed by the verb. There are three moods: *the indicative mood*, *the imperative mood* and *the subjunctive mood*.

The indicative mood

This is the mood of sentences that give facts.

> The dog **broke** the vase.

The imperative mood

The imperative mood is a command. Commands are always in the second person, because we are speaking directly to the person we want to carry out the command. To give a command, we simply use the *infinitive*, which is the basic form of the verb. We usually don't include the subject, because it is understood.

> **Come** inside and **eat** your dinner!

> **Give** me that CD!

> **Stop** making noise!

Commands can also be negative. To give a negative command, we add *do not* or *don't*:

> **Don't** do that!

> **Do not** go into the haunted house!

The subjunctive mood

This expresses some action as a doubt, possibility or wish. It is often used with the word *if* before the verb, and *would*, *could* or *should* after it.

> If I **were** you, I **wouldn't** miss that concert!

> If your cousin **should** come, he **would** be welcome.

> If I **were** a superhero, I **could** fly home from school!

In the examples above, you will see that the verb *were* is plural, even when the subject is singular. This is because the subjunctive mood changes the usual rules about subject/verb agreement.

I wish I **were** a movie star.

Voice

Voice tells us who is doing the action. Usually, the subject is the person or thing doing the action of the verb, but sometimes the subject actually has the action done to it.

There are two voices: *active* and *passive*.

- **Active voice**

  In the active voice, the subject does something to some person or thing.

John **climbed** the fence.	**Climbed** is a verb in the active voice because the subject (*John*) did something (**climbed**) to something (*the fence*).

- **Passive voice**

  In the passive voice, the subject receives the action. The passive voice is made up of a form of the verb *to be* plus the past participle of the main verb.

The fence **was climbed** by John.	**Was climbed** is a verb in the passive voice because the subject (*the fence*) had something done to it (**was climbed**) by someone (*John*). It is the subject, (*the fence*), that receives the action.

Verb phrase

A verb phrase is a group of words that contains a verb and any *auxiliary*, or helping, words, that it might have. It can be described as an *expanded verb*. A verb phrase can consist of a single word or number of words, such as *run* or *has been running*. (See Phrases, p. 38.)

Another type of verb phrase is a *phrasal verb*, which includes another word called a *particle*, such as *on* or *up*. The phrasal verb could be *jump on* or *catch up*.

Remember that verb phrases are still verbs. They tell us what is happening.

Verb group

A verb group is a word, or number of words, that does the job of a verb. Like noun groups, verb groups can be expanded.

In the following sentences, the verb groups are highlighted:

Jodie **runs**.

She **is running**.

Pierre **has not been running**.

They **could not have been running** .

The terms *verb groups* and *verb phrases* are sometimes combined under the term *group/phrase*. (See Groups, p. 38.)

The verb *to be*

The verb *to be* is a special verb. It has a number of meanings of its own (*to exist*, *to take place*, *to stay in the same place or condition*, etc.). It is also a very important *auxiliary*, or *helping*, verb.

The verb *to be* can show present, past and future tenses. It has more forms than any other verb in the English language.

Forms of the verb *to be*:

	Singular	Plural	Participle
Present	I **am** you **are** he/she/it **is**	we/you/they **are**	being
Past	I **was** you **were** he/she/it **was**	we/you/they **were**	been
Future	I **will be** you **will be** he/she/it **will be**	we/you/they **will be**	____

The verb *to be* can be an auxiliary verb, combining with other verbs to form the *continuous tenses*.

Present continuous tense: I **am riding** my bike.

Past continuous tense: He **was eating** his lunch.

Future continuous tense: She **will be going** home soon.

Compound and auxiliary verbs

Compound verbs are verbs that are made up of more than one word. They are made up from *auxiliary verbs* and *non-finite verbs* (infinitives or participles). They are also known as *verb phrases* or *verb groups*.

They **are going** to the movies.

John **had been helping** for some weeks.

Some auxiliary verbs that are used to show tense are:

have: I **have seen** a lion.

be: He **is looking for** his bag.

shall/will: I **will be finishing** work soon.

do: I **do not see** it that way.

I **have seen** a lion.
Auxiliary verb: have

Regular and irregular verbs

Most verbs form their tenses in a regular, or predictable, way.

Forms of the verb *to kick*:

	Singular	Plural	Participle
Present	I **kick** you **kick** he/she/it **kicks**	we/you/they **kick**	kicking
Past	I **kicked** you **kicked** he/she/it **kicked**	we/you/they **kicked**	kicked
Future	I **will kick** you **will kick** he/she/it **will kick**	we/you/they **will kick**	____

The important thing to remember is that the past tense and the past participle usually add the ending -*ed* to the infinitive. This ending may sometimes be shortened to -*d* or -*t*:

Infinitive	Past tense	Past participle
(to) learn	learned	learnt

Sometimes the past tense of the verb is the same as the past participle:

Infinitive	Past tense	Past participle
(to) spread	spread	spread

Where this occurs, the verb is said to be a *weak verb*.

Irregular verbs

Some verbs change their spelling in the past tense and past participle. These are called irregular verbs, because they do not follow the normal pattern. Irregular verbs are also called *strong verbs*.

Infinitive	Past tense	Past participle
(to) ring	rang	rung
(to) see	saw	seen
(to) do	did	done

Here are some common irregular verbs:

Infinitive	Past tense	Past participle
arise	arose	arisen
become	became	become
choose	chose	chosen
do	did	done
eat	ate	eaten
fly	flew	flown
give	gave	given
go	went	gone
know	knew	known
lie	lay	lain
ring	rang	rung
speak	spoke	spoken
take	took	taken
wear	wore	worn
write	wrote	written

REMEMBER

Don't confuse the past tense with the past participle! It's easy to get it right because the past participle is preceded by a part of another verb, usually the verb *to have*.

Past tense: *The bells **rang** last Sunday.*
Auxiliary plus past participle: *The bells **have rung** every Sunday this month.*
Do NOT say: *The bells ~~have rang~~.*

Say:	✓ *I saw the movie OR I have seen the movie.*
Don't say:	✗ *I ~~seen~~ the movie!*
Say:	✓ *I did it OR I have done it.*
Don't say:	✗ *I ~~done~~ it!*

Adverbs

An adverb adds meaning to, or modifies, verbs, adjectives and other adverbs.

An adverb is also called a *circumstance*, or part of a circumstance.

In the following sentences, the adverbs are highlighted:

I ran **quickly**.	**Quickly** is an adverb. It adds meaning to the verb *ran*—it tells *how* I ran.
I am a **very** fast runner.	In this sentence, **very** is an adverb. It adds meaning to the adjective *fast*—it tells *how fast* a runner I am.
You run **too** quickly for me.	In this sentence, **too** is an adverb. It adds meaning to the adverb *quickly*—it tells *how quickly* you run.

Types of adverbs

There are four main types of adverbs: *adverbs of manner*, *adverbs of time*, *adverbs of place* and *adverbs of reason*.

- Adverbs of manner tell *how* something is done:
  I walked **slowly.**
- Adverbs of time tell *when* something is done:
  I ran **yesterday.**
- Adverbs of place tell *where* something is done:
  I ran **there.**
- Adverbs of reason tell *why* something is done:
  Therefore I argue …

> **REMEMBER**
>
> Adverbs tell how, when, where and why.

There are other types of adverbs, too. It is important to learn how to recognise them.

- **Interrogative adverbs**
  An interrogative adverb is an adverb that asks a question. In the following sentences, the interrogative adverbs are highlighted:
  When did you get here?
  How are you?
  Where did she come from?
  Why are you laughing?

- **Negative adverbs**

  Negative adverbs are adverbs that make sentences negative. In the following sentences, the negative adverbs are highlighted:

  I do **not** agree.

  I will **not** do it!

  Never do that again!

Negative adverbs are often expressed as *contractions*. (See Apostrophes, p. 54.) The verb and the negative adverb are joined to make one shorter word:

  do not ➤ don't

  will not ➤ won't

  is not ➤ isn't

  have not ➤ haven't

- **Modal adverbs**

A modal adverb is an adverb that shows the amount of probability, certainty, ability or obligation in a sentence.

We will **probably** fly to the beach.
Modal adverb

Yes, probably, possibly, certainly and *definitely* are examples of modal adverbs. They are used to agree or to express doubt.

(See also Modal adjectives p. 15 and Modal verbs p. 19.)

- **Numerical adverbs**

  Numerical adverbs tell how often something took place:

    He called her **twice**.

- **Adverbs of degree**

  An adverb of degree tells us *to what extent* something happens:

    The train **almost** crashed.

    The plane flew **extremely** fast.

Words like *almost*, *hardly*, *enough* and *extremely* are adverbs of degree. They also tell us *how*, so they can be called *adverbs of manner*, too.

> **REMEMBER**
>
> Adverbs add meaning to verbs, adjectives and other adverbs. They do not add meaning to nouns.

Adverbs and the -ly ending

Many adverbs end in -ly.

    I can **hardly** see.   She is **nearly** ten.

Remember, though, that some -ly words can also be adjectives:

He was a **kindly** man.	In this sentence, **kindly** is an adjective, because it adds meaning to the noun *man*.
The **early** bird catches the worm.	In this sentence, **early** is an adjective, because it adds meaning to the noun *bird*.

You will always be able to tell the difference between adverbs and adjectives. Adverbs add meaning to verbs, adjectives and other adverbs. Adjectives only add meaning to nouns and pronouns.

More about adverbs

Adverbs and degree

Like adjectives, adverbs have three degrees of comparison: *positive*, *comparative* and *superlative*.

Adverbs with the *-ly* ending don't change their spelling to form the comparative and superlative, they simply add the adverbs *more* and *most*.

Positive	Comparative	Superlative
quietly	more quietly	most quietly
loudly	more loudly	most loudly
softly	more softly	most softly
clearly	more clearly	most clearly

Positive:	The dog howled **loudly**.
Comparative:	The wolf howled **more loudly**.
Superlative:	The dog howled **most loudly**!

Not all adverbs have the *-ly* ending. In fact, many look like adjectives. Some even form their comparative and superlative in the same way as adjectives—by adding the *-er* and *-est* endings.

Positive	Comparative	Superlative
hard	harder	hardest
long	longer	longest
early	earlier	earliest

> **REMEMBER**
>
> Some words can be adverbs and adjectives—it just depends on the job that they do in the sentence!

A few adverbs form degrees of comparison in an irregular way.

Positive	Comparative	Superlative
good	better	best
much	more	most
badly	worse	worst
good	better	best
big	bigger	biggest

Prepositions

A preposition is a positioning word, such as **in**, **on**, and **near**. It tells you the position of something.

Prepositions are usually found in front of nouns or pronouns to form a phrase:

on the table **near** him

Phrases like the ones above are called *prepositional phrases*. The preposition has a close relationship with the noun or pronoun that follows it.

on the table	The preposition **on** is related to the noun *table*.
near him	The preposition **near** is related to the pronoun *him*.

A preposition in a phrase governs the noun or pronoun in the *objective case*. This means that when a preposition is followed by a pronoun, the pronoun must be in the objective case: *me, him, her, us, them* or *whom*.

I gave the skateboard **to him**.	The preposition **to** is followed by the pronoun **him**. Him is in the objective case.
Dad shared the lollies **between** Mark and **me**.	The preposition **between** is followed by the noun *Mark* and the preposition **me**. **Me** is in the objective case.

Be careful with prepositional phrases involving the pronoun *me*. A lot of people make the mistake of saying or writing *I* when they should say or write *me*.
Don't say: ✘ Mum gave the toys to Sarah and I.
Say: ✔ Mum gave the toys to Sarah and **me**.
In the sentence above, the pronoun *me* is the object of the preposition *to*.
A good way to work out whether to use *I* or *me* is to take out the other people involved. If we take out *Sarah and*, we are left with:
Mum gave the toys to [Sarah and] me.

Prepositions are usually short words, although some, like **underneath**, are long.
Here are some common prepositions. There are many more.

across	beneath	into	over	before
after	between	like	past	in
among	during	near	to	on
around	from	of	up	with

More about prepositions

Special prepositions
Some prepositions are always used with certain nouns, adjectives, or verbs, or in certain phrases.

✔ We say: The team ran **onto** the pitch.

✘ Not: The team ran ~~into~~ the pitch.

You know which preposition to use in most cases because it sounds right when you say it. *We are pleased* **with** *things; we rely* **on** *things and we bring things* **under** *control.*

Some special prepositions need special attention.

We say:

✓ different **from**   ✓ **between** two   ✓ **among** three (or more)

Not:

✗ different **to**   ✗ **among** two   ✗ **between** three (or more)

✗ different **than**

Prepositions and adverbs

It is important not to confuse adverbs with prepositions. They may look exactly the same. You will know the difference because of the way the word is used.

I fell **down**.	In this sentence, **down** is an adverb of place; it tells *where* I fell.
I rowed **down** the river.	In this sentence, **down** is a preposition. It governs the noun **river**.

Another useful point to remember is that the preposition usually has a noun or pronoun after it.

I jumped **up**.	In this sentence, **up** is an adverb. It is not followed by a noun or preposition.
I ran **up** the hill.	In this sentence, **up** is a preposition. It is followed by the noun *hill*.

Note that the whole phrase, *up the hill*, does the job of an adverb and is called an *adverbial phrase*. It contains the preposition *up*.

Conjunctions

A conjunction is a joining word. Conjunctions help to hold texts together.

In the following sentences, the conjunctions are highlighted:

The bat hit the ball **and** the ball hit me.

I ate a sandwich **when** I got home from school.

Conjunctions help to link different parts of a sentence. They make the different parts *cohere*, or hold together. (See Cohesion, p. 60, Connectives, p. 61.)

There are two main types of conjunctions: *coordinating conjunctions* and *subordinating conjunctions*.

Coordinating conjunctions

A coordinating conjunction is a conjunction that links words, phrases or clauses that are grammatically 'equal'. That is, they are equally important to the meaning of a sentence.

I wore a hat **and** scarf to the snow.

I went skiing **but** didn't go tobogganing.

Coordinating conjunctions usually join the same or similar parts of a text together:

wet **and** cold   tired **but** happy   apple **or** pear

Coordinating conjunctions also join compound words and phrases:

Mary Jones **and** Pablo Lopes   on the beach **and** in the water

Coordinating conjunctions can also join separate sentences into a single sentence:

Without a conjunction: This is his book. That is her book.

With a conjunction: This is his book **and** that is her book.

Here are some common coordinating conjunctions:

and	but	for	nor
or	so	yet	

My aunt gave me a shirt **but** I didn't like it.
Coordinating conjunction

Subordinating conjunctions

Some conjunctions join parts of sentences called *clauses*. A subordinating conjunction is a conjunction that introduces a *subordinate clause*. (See Clauses, p. 42.)

A subordinate clause is dependent upon the main clause. It cannot exist without it.

I want to be a pilot **when** I grow up.

This sentence contains two clauses, *I want to be a pilot* and *when I grow up*.

The clause *when I grow up* is subordinate to, or dependent on, the clause *I want to be a pilot*. *When I grow up* doesn't make sense by itself. The word that joins the two clauses is *when*. This is called a subordinating conjunction.

Here are some common subordinating conjunctions:

after	before	though
whenever	although	once
unless	where	as
since	until	because
than	when	while

> **REMEMBER**
>
> A clause is a group of words that contains a finite verb and its subject. There can be more than one clause in a sentence.

More examples of subordinating conjunctions:

I'm all right **once** I get started.

I can't get into the house **until** Mum comes home.

This is the place **where** I go to school.

Correlative conjunctions

Some conjunctions exist in pairs. These conjunctions are called correlative conjunctions.

The most common correlative conjunctions are:

both … and	either … or
neither … nor	not only … but also
whether … or	not … but
as … as	

The batsman was **not only** stumped **but also** caught.

Neither Alberto **nor** Maria is in my class.

Articles

An article describes a noun and is a special kind of adjective.

There are only three articles:

the   a   an

The is called *the definite article*. *A* and *an* are called *indefinite articles*. (See Demonstrative adjectives, p. 14.)

The Pacific Ocean   **A** river   **An** ocean
Definite article   **Indefinite article**   **Indefinite article**

Definite article

The is the definite article. It is called definite because it refers to a particular thing or things.

The video game is really hard to complete!

I would like **the** steamed dumplings, please.

Indefinite article

A and **an** are indefinite articles. These articles refer to general, rather than particular, things.

Wear **a** coat, as it is very cold.

An owl is in the tree.

A coat refers to any coat, not a particular or special one. *An* refers to any owl, not a particular or special one.

A is used in front of a consonant: **a** coat

An is used in front of a vowel.   **an** owl

Interjections

An interjection is a word that is 'thrown in' to interrupt the flow of conversation or writing. Interjections usually express a strong feeling about something.

Ouch! That hurt.

Eek! What was that noise?

Ugh! I don't like tomato.
Interjection

Interjections are usually followed by an exclamation mark and, therefore, are types of exclamations.

Here are some examples of interjections:

Oh!   Oops!   Wow!

Ah!   Ouch!   Phew!

Parsing

The word *parsing* comes from the Latin word *pars* meaning 'part'. When you parse a sentence, you identify the name and function of each word. That is, you state the job that each word is doing.

Here is an example of parsing:

The hungry tiger watched them closely.

1. Start by naming each part of speech in the sentence:

The	hungry	tiger	watched	them	closely.
article	adjective	noun	verb	pronoun	adverb

2. Then, say what you know about each part of speech:

The	definite article
hungry	descriptive adjective modifying the noun *tiger*
tiger	common noun, third person; singular number; common gender (masculine or feminine); subjective case, subject of the verb *watched*
watched	transitive, finite verb; third person, singular number to agree with its subject, *tiger*; past tense, indicative mood, active voice
them	personal pronoun; third person; plural number; common gender; objective case after the verb *watched*
closely	adverb of manner modifying the verb *watched*

Today, we are more interested in the functions of words in a text as a whole, and how texts work in real-life situations.

Group, phrase, clause and sentence levels

Groups

A group is a word, or number of words, that has the function of a part of speech, such as a noun or a verb.

Noun group

A noun group is a word or number of words based upon a noun.

Here are some examples of noun groups:

dogs:	noun
the dogs:	article + noun
those dogs:	demonstrative adjective + noun
my dogs:	possessive adjective + noun
two dogs:	numeral adjective + noun
good dogs:	descriptive adjective + noun

Describing words that come before the noun are called *pre-modifiers*.

Describing words that come after the noun are called *post-modifiers*.

Noun groups function as nouns and can be expanded in many ways. They may even contain whole clauses.

The boy, **who liked to sing**, was excited about joining the choir.

The boy, who liked to sing,	(noun group)
who liked to sing	(adjectival clause within noun group)

Verb groups

A verb group is a word, or number of words, that does the job of a verb.

Here are some examples of verb groups:

jumps:	verb (simple present tense)
is jumping:	auxiliary verb + present participle (continuous present tense)
will be jumping:	auxiliary verbs + present participle (continuous future tense)
will not have been jumping:	negative auxiliary verbs + present participle (future perfect continuous tense)

Like noun groups, verb groups can be expanded in many ways.

Phrases

A phrase is a series of words that does not contain a finite verb and does not make sense by itself.

Phrases can do the work of different parts of speech, depending on how they function in texts.

Prepositional phrases

The most common phrase is the prepositional phrase. It begins with a preposition, which is followed by a noun group. Like all phrases, a prepositional phrase does not contain a finite verb.

in the water	In this prepositional phrase, **in** is the preposition, and **the water** is the noun group.
with my friends	In this prepositional phrase, **with** is the preposition, and **my friends** is the noun group.

We are **on the moon**!
Prepositional phrase

Adjectival phrases

Adjectival phrases are phrases that do the work of adjectives. Like adjectives, adjectival phrases add meaning to, describe or modify nouns or pronouns.

He was given the message **to be quiet**.	In this sentence, **to be quiet** is an adjectival phrase. It begins with an infinitive, **to be**, and modifies the noun *message*.
The cat, **drinking the cream**, was really enjoying her lunch.	In this sentence, **drinking the cream** is an adjectival phrase. It begins with a present participle, **drinking**, and modifies the noun *cat*.

Some adjectival phrases are also prepositional phrases. They begin with a preposition, which is followed by a noun group.

Elena is the girl **in the blue top**.	In this sentence, the adjectival phrase, **in the blue top**, describes the noun *girl*. It begins with a preposition, **in**, which is followed by a noun group, **the blue top**, so it is also a prepositional phrase.

Adverbial phrases

Adverbial phrases are phrases that do the work of adverbs. Like adverbs, they add meaning to, or modify, the action of verbs, adjectives and other adverbs. They tell *how*, *when*, *where* or *why* an action takes place.

I sat down **to have a rest**.	In this sentence, **to have a rest** is an adverbial phrase of reason. It begins with an infinitive, **to have**, and modifies the verb, *sat down*.

Some adverbial phrases are also prepositional phrases. They begin with a preposition, which is followed by a noun group.

I cut the ribbon **with the scissors**.	In this sentence, the adverbial phrase of manner, telling how you cut the ribbon, is **with the scissors**. It adds meaning to the verb, *cut*. It begins with a preposition, **with**, which is followed by a noun group, **the scissors**, so it is also a prepositional phrase.

There are four kinds of adverbial phrases.

- Adverbial phrases of manner tell *how* something is done.
- Adverbial phrases of time tell *when* something is done.
- Adverbial phrases of place tell *where* something is done.
- Adverbial phrases of reason tell *why* something is done.

Adverbial phrases of manner:

The dog was barking **in a threatening way**.

The adverbial phrase of manner is **in a threatening way**. It tells us *how* about the verb *was barking*.

Adverbial phrases of time:

Over the weekend, all the children play sport.

The adverbial phrase of time is **over the weekend**. It tells *when* about the verb *play*.

Adverbial phrases of place:

We often eat our lunch **on the school bus**.

The adverbial phrase of place is **on the school bus**. It tells *where* about the verb *eat*.

Adverbial phrases of reason:

We lost the game **because of the muddy ground**.

The adverbial phrase of reason is **because of the muddy ground**. It tells *why* about the verb *lost*.

Some adverbial phrases of reason begin with an infinitive:

They played hard **to win the game**.

The adverbial phrase of reason is **to win the game**. It tells *why* about the verb *played*. The phrase begins with the infinitive *to win*.

Noun phrases

A noun phrase is a phrase that does the work of a noun. It stands in place of a noun.

Playing football can be dangerous.

The phrase *playing football* stands in place of a noun, so it is a noun phrase.

Noun phrases usually begin with a *gerund* (verbal noun). (See Gerunds, p. 2.)

Noun phrases as the subject of the sentence

Sometimes, the subject of a sentence is a noun phrase. To find the subject, ask *Who?* or *What?* before the verb.

Patting stray dogs is dangerous.

Question: *What is dangerous?*

Answer: *Patting stray dogs.*

Patting stray dogs is a noun phrase because it acts like a noun, is the subject of the sentence and begins with the gerund *patting*. (See Gerunds, p. 2.)

Noun phrases as the object of the sentence

Sometimes, the object of a sentence is a noun phrase. To find the subject, ask *Who?* or *What?* after the verb.

> I love **eating baked beans**.
>
> **Question:** *Love what?*
>
> **Answer:** *Eating baked beans.*

Eating baked beans is a noun phrase because it acts like a noun, is the object of the sentence and begins with the gerund *eating*.

> **REMEMBER**
>
> The subject is the person or thing who performs the action of the verb.
> The object is the person or thing who has the action of the verb done to them.

More about phrases

Prepositional phrases and verbal phrases

Sometimes phrases are described by the part of speech they begin with, rather than the job they do in the sentence. If we look at them in this way, we could describe all phrases as either *prepositional phrases* or *verbal phrases*, depending on whether they begin with a preposition or a verb.

He sailed **on the boat**.	**On the boat** is a prepositional phrase. It begins with the preposition **on**, which is followed by the noun group **the boat**.
I saw the racing car, **painted bright red**.	**Painted bright red** is a verbal phrase, because it begins with the verb **painted**.

As we have seen, prepositional phrases begin with a preposition.

Verbal phrases can be divided into the following:

* Participial phrases, which begin with either a past or present participle:

  past participle: **painted** bright red

  present participle: **running** flat out

* Gerund phrases, which begin with a gerund (verbal noun):

  gerund: **skiing** down the mountain

* Infinitive phrases, which begin with an infinitive:

  Infinitive: **To watch** TV

But no matter how a phrase begins, it is the job the phrase does that is most important. To find out what type of phrase it is, it is very important to ask what it does.

* Is it an adjectival phrase?

  Does it do the job of an adjective? That is, does it add meaning to, modify or describe a noun?

The man **in the blue suit** coughed.	**In the blue suit** describes the noun *man*. It is an adjectival noun.

- Is it an adverbial phrase?

  Does it do the job of an adverb? Does it add meaning to, or modify, a verb, adjective or other adverb?

Maria dived **into the pool.**	**Into the pool** adds meaning to the verb *dived*. It is an adverbial phrase.

Clauses

A clause is a word or group of words that contains a finite verb and its subject.

To find the subject of the verb, ask *who?* or *what?* in front of the verb.

REMEMBER

A finite verb is a verb that has a subject.

Here are some examples of independent (principal) clauses:

Fish swim.	**Swim** is the finite verb and **fish** is the subject.
Fish swim in the sea.	**Swim** is the finite verb and **fish** is the subject. There is also a prepositional phrase, **in the sea**. This is an *adverbial phrase of place*, telling where fish swim.
Swim!	**Swim!** is the finite verb. The subject *you* is implied, or understood to be there in the sentence. This is an imperative. (See Understood subjects, p. 49, Imperatives, p. 26.)

A clause can also be described as a unit of meaning that gives a message. It tells us who or what is involved (noun group/phrase), what is happening (verb group/phrase) and what are the surrounding circumstances (adverb group/phrase). There can be more than one clause in a sentence.

Agreement of subject and verb

In a clause, the subject and the verb must agree. If the subject is singular, the verb must be singular, too.

This car is fast.

Singular subject	Singular verb	Adjective
The car	is	fast.

Those cars are fast.

Plural subject	Plural verb	Adjective
Those cars	are	fast.

The main clause

An independent clause is a clause that makes sense by itself. Because they make sense by themselves, independent clauses can also be sentences.

Independent clauses are also called *independent* or *principal clauses*.

Here are some examples of independent clauses. These clauses are also sentences:

Fish swim.

Fish swim in the sea.

Some sentences can contain two or more independent clauses. These clauses are joined by *coordinating conjunctions* and form a single sentence.

In the following sentence, there are two independent clauses, which are highlighted. The independent clauses are joined by the coordinating conjunction *and*.

Fish swim in the sea and **cows walk on the land.**

The subordinate clause

A subordinate clause adds meaning to the independent clause. It cannot exist without the independent clause.

A subordinate clause is also called a dependent clause, because it is dependent on the main (independent) clause. It cannot stand alone—it needs the dependent clause to make sense.

Fish can breathe underwater **because they have gills**.

This sentence contains two clauses, *Fish can breathe underwater* and *because they have gills*. The clause *because they have gills* is subordinate to, or dependent on, the clause *Fish can breathe underwater*.

Recognising independent and subordinate clauses

It is usually easy to recognise independent and subordinate clauses in sentences.

Look at the examples below. The independent clauses are <u>underlined</u> and the subordinate clauses are in a **box**.

<u>I saw him</u> **when I came in**.

<u>This is the boy</u> **who won the race** .

Watch out for an independent clause that is broken by another clause:

<u>The big red car,</u> **which I drove** , <u>won the race.</u>

In this sentence, the independent clause is *The big red car won the race.*

Types of subordinate clauses

Subordinate clauses are described by the same name as the parts of speech that could take their place. They do the same job.

(See Subordinating conjunctions, p. 35.)

Adverbial clauses

An adverbial clause does the work of an adverb. It adds meaning to a verb, an adjective or an adverb.

I ate my breakfast **after I had a shower** .   **After I had a shower** tells *when* I ate my breakfast, so it does the work of an adverb. It is an adverbial clause of time.

Adverbial clauses begin with subordinating conjunctions. Here are some examples of subordinating conjunctions:

after   although   as   because   since   until   when   while

Like adverbs, there are adverbial clauses of *manner*, *time*, *place* and *reason*. These tell *how*, *when*, *where* and *why*.

- Adverbial clauses of manner tell *how*: You may do as you please .
- Adverbial clauses of time tell *when*: We cheered when they arrived .
- Adverbial clauses of place tell *where*: They fish where the water is deep .
- Adverbial clauses of reason tell *why*:

  I'll have strawberry ice cream because it is my favourite .

Other types of adverbial clauses are:

- Comparison: It is not as valuable as it looks .
- Concession: I fed the cat although it scratched me .
- Condition: I will meet him if he is on time .
- Degree or comparison: The girl could run as fast as a hare .
- Purpose: They went to the beach so that they could surf .
- Result: He ran so fast that he won the race .

Adjectival clauses

An adjectival clause does the work of an adjective. It adds meaning to a noun.

This is the cat that killed the rat .   **That killed the rat** adds meaning to the noun *cat*, so it does the work of an adjective. It is an adjectival clause.

An adjectival clause begins with a relative pronoun. The relative pronouns are:

who   whom   which   that

(See Relative pronouns, p. 9.)

Another example of an adjectival clause is:

He spoke to the woman who was watching the cricket .

Some adjectival clauses might be more difficult to recognise.

In the following example, the independent clause is separated:

The snow, which fell all night , was very deep.

In the following example, the adjectival clause appears not to begin with a relative pronoun. But in this case, the word *where* actually means *at which*. So the clause is an adjectival clause describing the noun *place*.

This is the place where we will have lunch .

Embedded clauses

An embedded clause is a subordinate, or dependent, clause within a main (independent) clause. The embedded clause becomes part of the noun group and helps to define the noun.

The house **that Jack built.**

The girl **who had long hair** won the prize.

Restrictive (defining) and non-restrictive (non-defining) clauses

There is a distinction between these two types of clauses. Restrictive clauses help to define the main noun in the noun group. Non-restrictive clauses do not.

This is important because restrictive, or defining, clauses are embedded, while non-restrictive, or non-defining, clauses are not.

Restrictive and non-restrictive clauses can look very similar, but the meaning of the sentences they belong to are different.

Restrictive clause: Jack ate the apples $\boxed{\text{that were green}}$.

In this sentence, the clause *that were green* is restrictive (defining) and *embedded*. It defines the noun *apples*, providing essential information. The sentence could be rewritten as: *Jack ate the green apples*. There may have been other apples, but *Jack* only ate the green ones.

Non-restrictive clause: Jack ate the apples, $\boxed{\text{which were green}}$.

In this sentence, the clause *which were green* is non-restrictive, and not embedded. It does not define the noun *apples*, and does not provide essential information. The sentence could be rewritten as *Jack ate the apples*. It didn't matter what colour they were, Jack ate them anyway!

The difference between the two sentences is shown in the use of the different relative pronouns, *that* and *which*. In the second sentence, there is also a comma. This shows that the clause is non-restrictive and not embedded. If you were to say the two sentences out loud, you would say each one a little bit differently. Try it! (See Commas, p. 53, Relative pronouns, p. 9.)

Noun clauses

A noun clause does the work of a noun. It can be either the subject or object of a verb.

$\boxed{\text{What they saw}}$ was amazing.

What they saw is a noun clause, the subject of the verb *was*.

I know $\boxed{\text{that the apples are juicy}}$.

That the apples are juicy is a noun clause, the object of the verb *know*.

If a noun clause comes after a part of the verb *to be*, it is said to be the *complement* of the verb. The verbs *seem*, *become*, *remain*, *look* and *appear* also take complements.

That is $\boxed{\text{what I ordered}}$.

What I ordered is a noun clause, the complement of the verb **is**.

Sometimes, a noun clause can be the object of a preposition.

I sold the book for $\boxed{\text{what it was worth}}$.

What it was worth is a noun clause, the object of the preposition **for**.

Noun clauses are often introduced by *that*:

I saw $\boxed{\text{that the ship had arrived}}$.

That the ship had arrived is a noun clause, object of the verb *saw*.

But sometimes *that* is omitted:

I told him $\boxed{\text{the cake was cooked}}$.

The cake was cooked is a noun clause, the object of the verb *told*.

Noun clauses can be introduced by other words as well. Just remember that the type of clause depends on the job or function of the clause in the sentence.

I told him $\boxed{\text{who won the prize}}$.

Who won the prize is a noun clause, the object of the verb *told*.

I know $\boxed{\text{where the dog is hiding}}$.

Where the dog is hiding is a noun clause, the object of the verb *know*.

Sentences

A sentence is a group of words that contains a finite verb and has a complete meaning. It tells us what is happening and who or what is taking part.

The girls are playing netball.

Ask: Who is taking part?	**The girls**	(noun group)
Ask: What is happening?	**are playing**	(verb group)
	netball	(noun group)

A sentence can contain surrounding circumstances and details.

The girls are playing netball in the park.

Circumstance: **In the park**   (adverbial phrase of place)

There are different types of sentences.

Statement, or declarative sentences, simple sentences

A statement deals with facts or ideas. We can describe the key parts of a statement as the *subject* and *predicate*.

The subject is found by asking *who?* or *what?* in front of the verb.

The predicate consists of the finite verb and everything that follows it. You find the predicate by asking *who* or *what* after the verb.

The cat has drunk the milk.

Ask: Who?	**The cat**
Ask: What has the cat done?	**has drunk the milk**

The cat is the subject and **has drunk the milk** is the predicate.

Questions

With questions, we change the order of the words. The auxiliary verb comes first, then the subject, then the rest of the verb group.

The cat **has** drunk the milk. → **Has** the cat drunk the milk?

If there is no auxiliary verb, we have to invent one by using *do*, *does* or *did*.

He plays tennis. → **Does** he play tennis?

Sometimes when speaking, we simply raise our voice at the end to ask a question.

The cat drank the milk?

> **REMEMBER**
>
> An auxiliary verb is a verb that is used with other verbs or participles to complete a verb. For example, 'I **have** seen that movie.'

Yes or No questions

These are questions that can be answered with '*yes*' or '*no*'. They are also called *closed questions*, because they don't require the person answering to give any extra information.

Question: Are you happy today?   **Answer:** Yes.

Question: Does your dog like storms? **Answer:** No.

Wh- questions

Wh- questions require a longer answer than just '*yes*' or '*no*'. These types of questions are called *open questions* and begin with words like *who*, *when* and *where*. *Wh-* questions cannot be answered with *yes* or *no*.

The *wh-* words are called interrogative words. These are interrogative words:

who   whose   whom   which   what   when   where   why

The tag question

The tag question is used mainly in speech, to confirm something that is more or less expected to be true.

Tag questions confirm something that the speaker already knows, or believes to be true:

You shut the door, didn't you?

In the tag sentence above, the speaker already knows that the person being spoken to has shut the door. *Didn't you?* is the tag and the whole sentence is a tag question. The speaker really believes that the door is shut but is just checking!

Commands

A command has a simple structure. To give a command, we simply use the *infinitive*, which is the basic form of the verb. The subject is always second person (you), but we don't need to include it, because it's understood. (See Imperative mood, p. 26, and Understood subjects, p. 49.)

Here are some commands:

Run!

Jump into bed.

Eat your vegetables.

Commands can also be negative:

Don't laugh!

Do not walk on the grass.

Exclamations

An exclamation is used to express a strong feeling about something—fear, surprise, happiness, etc. When we write, we can use an exclamation mark to indicate that we are exclaiming, or calling out. When we speak, we can put emphasis on different parts of the exclamation. (Try it!)

Here are some exclamations:

It was great fun!   I was amazed!   It was so scary!

We can also use a different form of expression, such as:

* *How* plus an adjective: **How** wonderful!
* *What* plus a noun group: **What** a crazy plan!

Compound/combined sentences

Sometimes two or more main clauses are joined by a *coordinating conjunction* to form a compound sentence. Because the clauses are independent, they will each have a *predicate* (which includes a finite verb) and a subject.

The cat ran and the dog chased after it.

This compound sentence has two main clauses. The first is *The cat ran*, and the second is *the dog chased after it*.

* **First independent clause:**   **The cat ran**
  Finite verb: ran
  Subject: The cat

| Predicate: | ran |
| Coordinating conjunction: | and |

- **Second independent clause:** **the dog chased after it**
  Finite verb: chased
  Subject: the dog
  Predicate: chased after it

In the following compound sentences, the finite verbs are highlighted and the main/independent clauses are underlined.

Dad mowed the lawn and Mum weeded the garden.

The phone rang but no one answered it.

Complex sentences

Complex sentences have a *main clause* and a *subordinate clause*. The subordinate clause begins with a subordinating conjunction or a relative pronoun. (See Clauses, p. 42.)

The cat knew when it was in danger.

This complex sentence has a main clause, *The cat knew*, and a subordinate clause, *when it was in danger*.

- **Independent clause:** **The cat knew**
  Finite verb: knew
  Subject: The cat
  Predicate: knew
  Subordinating conjunction: when

- **Subordinate clause:** **when it was in danger**
  Finite verb: was
  Subject: it
  Predicate: was in danger

In the following complex sentences, the finite verbs are highlighted. The principal clause is underlined and the subordinate clause is in a box.

The car was very old so Dad sold it.

The kite, which I was given for my birthday, flew really high.

Compound/complex sentences

Some sentences can be both compound and complex:

She went running and took her dog, which was a Labrador.

Using sentences

We use different types of sentences for different purposes:

- We use statements to give us information or present ideas: *I think it might rain.*
- We use questions to ask for information: *Are you going to the beach?*
- We use commands to tell someone to do something: *Swim between the flags.*
- We use exclamations to exclaim, to call out: *How delicious! What a pain!*

More about sentences

Understood subjects

Some sentences don't seem to have a subject.

> Go away!

This sentence is a command. The verb is *go*. When we ask *who?* or *what?* in front of the verb, we don't seem to get an answer.

When we say *Go away!* we are referring to *you*, even though the word *you* is not written. When this occurs, we can say that *you* is understood. In other words, the sentence is really saying:

> **(You)** go away!

As we have now found the subject, we can say that the verb *go* in this sentence is a *finite verb* because it has a subject. (See Commands, p. 47.)

The following sentences also have a subject that is understood.

Throw that away!	**Subject:** *you*
Help!	**Subject:** *you*

Negative statements, questions and commands

To make statements and questions negative, insert the word *not* after the auxiliary verb.

> She has played. → She has **not** played.

You can also shorten the auxiliary + *not* using the ending *-n't*.

> Has she played? → **Hasn't** she played?

do not → do**n't**

did not → did**n't**

does not → does**n't**

have not → have**n't**

has not → has**n't**

could not → could**n't**

If there is no auxiliary verb, make one up! Use *do*, *done*, or *did* with the verb.

> It hurts. → It **does not** hurt.   or   It **doesn't** hurt.

To make a command negative, we also add an auxiliary verb:

> Run! → **Don't** run!

Punctuating sentences

Sentence punctuation can vary according to the form of the sentence, although all sentences have some things in common. The four forms of the sentence are *statement*, *question*, *command* and *exclamation*. (See Punctuation, p. 51-8.)

- All sentences begin with a capital letter:

  We are going on a holiday. We're going to the Great Barrier Reef.

- Statements end with a full stop:

  She is my friend. We like going to the park together.

- Questions end with a question mark:

  Is Alanna still my friend?

- Commands often end with a full stop. They can also end with an exclamation mark:

  Get away from that mud.

  Don't sit there!

- Exclamations end with an exclamation mark:

  You're joking!

Commas are important in sentences. They help to make the meaning clearer, and can be used to change the meaning. Notice the difference in meaning between these two sentences:

  I read the books that I liked.

  I read the books, which I liked.

The first sentence means: *I read only the books that I liked (and no others)*. The second sentence means: *I read (all) the books and I liked them.* (See Embedded clauses, p. 44, and Restrictive and non-restrictive clauses p. 44.)

Analysis of sentences

Finding and naming the clauses in sentences is called analysis. Analysis involves saying what you know about each clause. It often goes with *parsing*, which involves saying what you know about each part of speech in a sentence. (See Parsing, p. 37.)

Although most teachers today would not analyse sentences completely, analysis tells you how many clauses there will be in the sentence or passage.

How to analyse a sentence

Begin by underlining the finite verbs:

  I <u>saw</u> the whale and I <u>saw</u> the calf. The whale, which <u>was</u> very large, <u>was</u> swimming slowly. I <u>knew</u> that the calf <u>was</u> nearby, because they always <u>swam</u> together.

There are three sentences in this passage. Let's look at each sentence separately:

Sentence 1:	*I <u>saw</u> the whale and I <u>saw</u> the calf.*
Main/independent clause:	I saw the whale
Main/independent clause:	I saw the calf
Sentence 2:	*The whale, which <u>was</u> very large, <u>was</u> swimming slowly.*
Principal/independent clause:	The whale was swimming slowly
Adjectival clause (qualifying whale):	which was very large
Sentence 3:	*I <u>knew</u> that the calf <u>was</u> nearby, because they always <u>swam</u> together.*
Principal/independent clause:	I knew
Noun clause (object of knew):	that the calf was nearby
Adverbial clause of reason (modifying was):	because they always swam together

I swam with the whales.
Principal clause

Punctuation

Capital letters

Capital letters are used as the first letter for all proper nouns.

Brian   London   Pacific Ocean

Titles of special people also take capital letters:

Captain Smith   Father John   Councillor Yeung

> **REMEMBER**
>
> A proper noun is the special name of a person, place or thing.

The personal pronoun *I* is always written with a capital letter:

I   I'd   I'll   I'm   I've

A capital letter is used as the first letter of the first word of every sentence:

My dog's name is Bill. He is a cocker spaniel.

The main words in the title of a book, a play, a film, a television show and many headings start with capital letters.

Harry Potter and the Philosopher's Stone

Wide World of Sport

When writing *direct speech*, a capital letter is used at the beginning of the first word in quotation marks.

'It's heavy,' said Grandma.

Robin asked, 'How do you get there?'

However, if a sentence is broken up by the words used to explain direct speech, the second part of that sentence does not take a capital letter.

'It's good,' said Joan, 'to come back home after a holiday.'

Full stops

A full stop is used at the end of most sentences.

Statement sentence:	The cat chased the rat.
	The rat ran as fast as it could.
Command sentence:	Bring the ball back here.

Shortened forms of words

Sometimes words or groups of words are written in a shortened form. There are four main types of shortened forms: *abbreviations, contractions, initialisms* and *acronyms*. Full stops were traditionally used in all shortened forms, but nowadays they are only used in abbreviations.

- Abbreviations shorten a word so that only the first letter and part of the rest of the word is used. The last letter is not used. A full stop is used to show that part of the word is missing.

Major → Maj.   Captain → Capt.

etcetera → etc.   figure → fig.

- Contractions shorten a word so that the first letter, the last letter and often some other parts of the word are used. Contractions do not need a full stop.

  Mister ➤ **Mr**

  Mistress ➤ **Mrs**

  Doctor ➤ **Dr**

  Avenue ➤ **Ave**

- Initialisms use only the first letters of each word in a group of words. Words that are not important are often left out. Initialisms do not need a full stop.

  United States of America ➤ **USA**

  Western Australia ➤ **WA**

  Australian Capital Territory ➤ **ACT**

  New South Wales ➤ **NSW**

  Member of Parliament ➤ **MP**

- Acronyms are initialisms that make a new word. Acronyms do not need full stops.

  Australian and New Zealand Army Corps ➤ **ANZAC**

  United Nations International Children's Emergency Fund ➤ **UNICEF**

  Self-contained Underwater Breathing Apparatus ➤ **scuba**

  Light Amplification by Stimulated Emission of Radiation ➤**laser**

Question marks

A question mark is also used at the end of a sentence that is a question.

Are you coming to school tomorrow?

A question mark can be used in the middle of a sentence to show that the writer is unsure of the information or the spelling contained in that sentence. The question mark shows this uncertainty.

The race will be held over the long weekend (?) if there are enough starters.

It was a weird (?) film.

(See Direct quotations with question marks, p. 57.)

Exclamation marks

An exclamation mark is used when the writer wants to show strong feelings about a person or event. That feeling might be excitement, surprise, anger, disappointment etc.

What a surprise!

Yuck!

(See Direct quotations with exclamation marks, p. 57.)

Some sentences look like questions but are really exclamations. If the speaker requires an answer, then the sentence is a question. But if an answer is not required, the sentence is probably an exclamation.

Will you have a look at that!

Isn't my hat beautiful!

Exclamation is a sentence.

Commas

A comma is used in a sentence to give a short pause. Commas help to make the meaning clearer by separating parts of the sentence.

Commas and lists

Commas are used to separate items in a list:

Julia had a dog, a cat, a budgie and a goldfish as pets.

In this list, the last pet is a *goldfish*. It is preceded by the word *and*. In cases such as these, there is no need for a comma.

If the list includes longer phrases a comma before *and* will sometimes make the meaning clearer.

James had a bike, a scooter, a skateboard, a surfboard, and a pair of roller blades.

Commas with adjectives and adverbs

Commas are used when we have two or more adjectives modifying a noun, or two or more adverbs modifying a verb.

Jane is a bright, happy, cheerful student.

Grant silently, slowly, carefully moved towards the door.

Commas with compound sentences

When two main (independent) clauses are joined by a coordinate conjunction (*and, but, or, nor, for, so, yet*) to form a compound sentence, a comma can be used to separate the clauses. Many writers would not use a comma.

I was going to come earlier, but I had to finish my homework.

Or

I was going to come earlier but I had to finish my homework.

If the two principal clauses are short, there is no need for a comma.

I missed the train **so** I caught the bus.

Commas with connectives, phrases and clauses beginning a sentence

Some sentences begin with a *connective* such as *so* or *however*. A comma should be used to separate the connective from the rest of the sentence.

However, I still think you are wrong.

Sentences often begin with a phrase or a clause. A comma is usually placed after the phrase or clause.

In the cool of the morning, we set off to find the old mine.

Although Jan was very late, Edward decided he would wait for her.

Commas separating words, phrases and clauses within sentences

Commas are used to separate words, phrases or clauses that occur within the sentence. These words may add extra information, but they don't change the meaning of the sentence.

Mr Caldwell, our new coach, used to be a professional footballer.

Nikola, who has just had a birthday, is coming here for dinner.

> ## Commas can change meaning!
>
> Using commas when giving extra information is important. They change the meaning of your sentences.
>
> *Anna ate the apples that were green.*
>
> *Anna ate the apples, which were green.*
>
> (See Embedded clauses and Restrictive and non-restrictive clauses, p. 44.)

Apostrophes

An apostrophe is used to show that letters have been left out of a contraction.

cannot → can't   it is → it's

will not → won't   you are → you're

he is → he's

Apostrophes are also used to show ownership with nouns.

the man's hat

the children's books

the ladies' lunches

> ### REMEMBER
>
> There's an easy way to work out where you place the apostrophe showing ownership. When something is owned, place the apostrophe after the last letter of the owner. This rule always works. **the ten athletes' feet**
> The athletes own the feet, so the apostrophe goes after the **s** in *athletes*.

If two or more people share ownership, only the last owner has an apostrophe.

Tim and Mary**'s** house.

If two or more people each own something, each owner has an apostrophe.

Tim**'s** and Mary**'s** noses.

An apostrophe is often used to show the plurals of numbers and letters.

seven s's   four 4's   Mind your p's and q's.

> ### REMEMBER
>
> A lot of people make mistakes when using apostrophes and pronouns. But it's easy to remember how to use them correctly!
> If you are using a pronoun to show possession, don't use an apostrophe.
> *That is his book.   This cake is hers.   The dog chewed its bone.*
> The only time you should use an apostrophe with a pronoun is when there are letters left out of a contraction.
> *You're [You + are] very clever!   It's [It + is] going to rain today.*

Apostrophes and pronouns

Some pronouns need apostrophes.

one**'s** foot   another**'s** feet

Possessive pronouns ending in **s** do not have an apostrophe. This is because the possession is already built into the pronoun:

his   hers   its   ours   yours   theirs

This is hers and that is yours.

I saw its furry tail.

It's is not a possessive. It is the contraction of *it is*.

Semicolons

A semicolon is mostly used between two connected or balanced ideas in a sentence. It is often described as a stop between a comma and a full stop. A semicolon can often be replaced by inserting a full stop and starting a new sentence, but this does not show the link between the two parts as strongly as a semicolon.

I enjoy swimming; it's such fun.

Don't go near the polar bears; they could eat you up!

Semicolon used to connect two ideas

> **REMEMBER**
>
> Do not use a semicolon to join a principal clause to a clause or phrase.
>
> ✗ **Don't write:** *He gave me the sandwich; although I didn't want it.*
> In this sentence, a comma or no punctuation should be used. Use a comma after a phrase or clause (see p. 53).
> ✓ **Write:** *He gave me the sandwich, although I didn't want it.*

Semicolons can be used with connecting words like *however, moreover, nevertheless, then* and *therefore*.

The two dogs are of the same breed; however, they have different personalities.

First we went to the theatre; then we visited the art gallery.

Use a semicolon when you want to separate a list of long items.

I saw the film about wildlife in America; the one about the Sahara Desert; and that one with all the snakes and lizards in it.

Semicolons are often used at the ends of lines of poetry.

One, two,	Pick up sticks;
Buckle my shoe;	Seven, eight,
Three, four,	Lay them straight;
Knock at the door;	Nine, ten,
Five, six,	A good fat hen.

A semicolon can be used when a comma would be confusing.

The words can be used in paragraphs, sentences or phrases; or by themselves.

Colons

A colon introduces more information. The information can be a list, words, phrases or clauses, or a quotation.

The following clothes should be taken on the trip: a warm jacket, a pullover, three pairs of socks, a pair of jeans, a change of underwear and a strong pair of shoes.

The warning read: 'Give up hope all ye who enter here.'

Brackets

Brackets, also known as parentheses, are always used in pairs. They enclose extra information such as an example, a comment or an explanation.

Buy a kilogram of fish (bream) and a bag of potatoes.

Carlos (a friend of mine) was there.

Volleyball (a game played on a court) is very good exercise.

Brackets used to enclose extra information

Dashes

Dashes are like brackets; they enclose extra information. However, they do not have to be in pairs.

Have an orange—or would you prefer a peach?

Dashes and brackets are used to show sudden changes in thought.

I have this friend—oops, there's the bell—who is in Year Six.

A dash can be used to show that something being said has been broken off.

I really would like—

Hyphens

A hyphen links two or more words or word parts that have to do the job of one.

reddish-brown coat   ten-year-old girl

Here are some examples of how to use hyphens:

- with a prefix when the main word starts with a capital letter:

  trans-Pacific

- with special prefixes:

  self-control   re-enter

- to make the meaning clear:

  Re-creation means created again.

  Recreation means a sport or pastime.

- with fractions and whole numbers:

  three-eighths   nine-tenths   twenty-five

- to form compound adjectives (adjectives made up of two or more words):

  greyish-white colour   well-known author

- to form some compound nouns:

  brother-in-law   jack-of-all-trades

Always consult your dictionary to check the use of hyphens in words if you are not sure.

Ellipses

The points of ellipsis indicate that something has been left out. They are useful when you are writing a play or a story.

'I wish ...' he said.

Quotations and punctuation

A quotation is a word or group of words that are repeated. The repeated words can come from speech or from something that is written.

There are two main forms of quotation: *direct quotation* and *indirect quotation*.

Quotations can use all of the different kinds of punctuation marks that we have covered. They also have their own punctuation marks—*quotation marks*, which are also known as *inverted commas* or *speech marks*. Speech marks are used with direct quotations.

Direct quotations and quotation marks

A direct quotation repeats what someone has said or written exactly as they said or wrote it. Direct quotations are often called *direct speech*.

Direct quotations use verbs that tell us about the quotation. These verbs are part of the sentence that surrounds the quotation. They include words like *said, wrote, shouted, whispered*, etc.

'I love birthdays!' **said** Grandma.

'All's well that ends well,' **wrote** Shakespeare.

Direct quotations use quotation marks to indicate the words being repeated. Quotation marks always come in pairs—the opening quotation mark goes at the beginning of the quotation, and the closing quotation mark goes at the end.

'I like juicy apples,' said Mary.

'A stitch in-time saves nine' is a useful proverb.

Sometimes double quotation marks are used:

"My dog needs a bath," said Luke.

Sometimes single quotation marks are used:

'My dog needs a bath,' said Luke.

It doesn't matter which you use. The important thing is to be consistent—don't switch from single quotation marks to double quotation marks!

Sometimes, a quotation contains another quotation. We use one type of quotation marks for the first quotation, and the other kind for the second quotation.

"I heard her say, 'I like juicy apples'," said Jim.

Or:

'I heard her say, "I like juicy apples",' said Jim.

Titles of books, poems and other special names often require quotation marks around them.

He read 'The Hobbit'.

The teacher read 'The Man from Snowy River' to the class.

Nowadays, we can use italics on our computers instead of quotation marks for the titles of books and movies.

I really enjoyed *Spiderman*!

Direct quotations with full stops

Full stops are often replaced with commas in direct quotations. But they are used to end the sentence that reports the direct quotation. (See Direct quotations and commas, p. 58.)

'Don't you like baths?' asked Luke.

'I think I'll go for a swim,' said Chantal.

In the sentence above, the full stop that would normally end the sentence *I think I'll go for a swim* has been replaced with a comma, because the direct quotation is part of a bigger sentence. The full stop goes where the sentence actually ends, which is after the word *Chantal*.

Direct quotations with question marks

When a direct quotation (direct speech) includes a question, the question mark is placed straight after the question, inside the quotation marks.

Dad asked, 'What would you like for dinner?'

Often, the question being quoted is not at the end of the sentence. The question mark is still used at the end of the reported speech, and then a full stop is used at the end of the sentence.

'Whose bag is that?' asked the teacher.

Direct quotations with exclamation marks

The rules for exclamation marks in direct quotations are the same as the rules for question marks in direct quotations. The exclamation mark is placed straight after the exclamation, inside the quotation marks.

'What a disaster!' exclaimed the coach.

When the exclamation being quoted is not at the end of the sentence, the exclamation mark is used at the end of the quote, and then a full stop is used at the end of the sentence.

'You are a great dog!' said Luke.

Direct quotations and commas

Commas are used to separate a quotation from the rest of the sentence that contains it.

- When the quotation comes at the start of the sentence—and it is not a question or an exclamation—a comma is used at the end of the quotation but before the *closing* quotation mark. This is followed by the words used to explain direct speech—*said, answered, replied, asked* etc.

  'I'm all right,' I said.

- When the quotation comes at the end of the sentence, a comma is used after the words used to explain direct speech, but before the *opening* quotation mark.

  I said, 'I'm all right.'

Because the quoted sentence is a statement, it ends with a full stop, which is placed before the closing quotation mark.

- When a statement is interrupted by the words used to explain direct speech, those words are enclosed by commas.

  'I am ready,' he said, 'to do what you ask me to do.'

- When the quotation is a question or an exclamation, we use a question mark or an exclamation mark at the end of the quotation, but before the closing quotation mark. We don't need to use a comma.

  'Is that you, Tom?' I asked.   'Ouch!' he cried.

- Where a question or exclamation is interrupted by the words used to explain direct speech, those words are enclosed by commas, and the question mark or the exclamation mark is used at the end of the quotation but before the closing quotation mark.

  'Do you think,' she asked, 'that I could have a glass of water?'

Indirect quotations

An indirect quotation tells what someone has said or written, but does not necessarily use exactly the same words.

Direct quotation:	'I don't want an ice cream,' said Mia.
Indirect quotation:	Mia said that she didn't want an ice cream.

In the first example, we are given Mia's words exactly as she said them. In the second example, we are told what she said, but not using her exact words.

Indirect quotations do not use quotation marks. They are often introduced by the word *that*.

Indirect quotations are statement sentences, which means that they usually end with a full stop. Sometimes, they might end with an exclamation mark.

Indirect quotations that report a question or an exclamation do not need a question mark or an exclamation mark.

Direct quotation:	'Will you come for a swim?' I asked Molly.
Indirect quotation:	I asked Molly if she would come for a swim.
Direct quotation:	'The concert was excellent!' said Amina.
Indirect quotation:	Amina said that the concert was excellent.

Text level

Text level structure

The text, whether spoken or written, goes beyond word level, group/phrase level and sentence level. The text level refers to the structure, or make-up, of a particular text type, such as a narrative or a procedure. It also refers to the structure of paragraphs and the way the whole text coheres, or holds together. (See Cohesion, pp. 65-6.)

When we understand how a text is put together, and how it differs from other texts, we are better able to understand it and write another text like it.

Text differences

There are a number of different text types, and they are all quite different from one another. (See pp. 68-88.) For instance, a *narrative*, which is a literary text type, tells a story and contains different characters. It is made up of an orientation that sets up the scene of the story, then the story itself, with its complication, and the final resolution. In a narrative there are many different examples of grammar at the various levels: proper nouns, action verbs, different clauses, sentence types, paragraphs and a host of other different grammatical features.

A *procedure*, on the other hand, is a factual text type, not a literary one. It contains a goal, a list of the things needed, and the steps or instructions that show the reader what to do. In a procedure you will find commands, action verbs, adverbial phrases and connectives, such as *first* and *next*.

Paragraphs

Written texts can be divided into *paragraphs*. Paragraphs are little 'chunks' or bundles of information that deal with a main idea or ideas in a text. They usually consist of a number of sentences. Each paragraph typically has a *topic sentence* that pinpoints the main idea.

Here is an example of paragraphs in an *exposition*, which is a type of persuasive text.

Nuts are good for you

Paragraph 1	**Nuts are good for you.** They are a rich source of protein and other important nutrients. These include unsaturated fats, amino acids, vitamins and potassium. However, there is a wrong way and a right way to eat nuts.	*Topic sentence* (Nuts are good for you)
Paragraph 2	**Here is the wrong way: eating nuts as an extra to your usual intake of meals and snacks will make you put on weight.** It could add another five kilos or more to your body weight over a year.	*Topic sentence* (Here is the wrong way …)
Paragraph 3	**Here is the right way: eat nuts instead of chips or sweets for a snack.** Include nuts as part of your usual lunch and eat them instead of meat for your main meal. They make delicious dishes. Nuts are good for you, there's no doubt!	*Topic sentence* (Here is the right way …)

The topic sentence

The topic sentence summarises the main idea in a paragraph. It is usually at the beginning of the paragraph. The remainder of the paragraph expands on the topic sentence. In the case of an exposition or discussion, it presents the points that support it.

Look at the exposition, *Nuts are good for you*. You will see that the topic sentences clearly lay out the main idea discussed in each paragraph.

Theme

(See Theme and Rheme, p. 65.)

The theme of a clause directs the flow of information and places focus on the idea that is to be developed. It is a signal for the reader.

The rheme is the remainder of the clause—everything but the theme.

In the exposition, *Nuts are good for you*, the first sentence is *Nuts are good for you*. The theme of this sentence is *nuts,* and the rheme is the rest of the clause. The emphasis is on *nuts* as it comes first.

Here are some examples of theme patterns in different text types:

Narrative:	Once upon a time …
Exposition:	Secondly, it is argued …
Procedure:	Slice … stir …
Recount:	Afterwards, we …

Cohesion

(See Cohesion, pp. 65-6.)

Cohesion forms links, or *cohesive ties*, that hold a text together.

There are many ways the links are formed. They include *reference ties*, *substitution*, *conjunctions* and others. All of the devices that make the text cohere are important and make the text an interconnected whole.

Further text links

Other text links are formed by words that have association with one another.

Repetition

Repetition forms links through the repeating of words or groups of words.

Kangaroos are marsupials. **Kangaroos** carry their young in pouches.
Kangaroos move by …

Synonyms

Synonyms are words that have the same or similar meaning, such as *laugh* and *chuckle*; *leap* and *jump*; *sleep* and *slumber*.

Antonyms

Antonyms are words that have opposite meanings, such as *hot* and *cold*; *fast* and *slow*; *wet* and *dry*.

Collocation

Collocation is a general, wider term used for words that usually go together, or *co-locate*, such as *kitchen, bedroom, bathroom, sitting room, rumpus room* and *study*. They may include some of the linking devices outlined on the previous page or others, such as *word sets* or *clusters*.

Word sets, chains, word families

Whole to part:

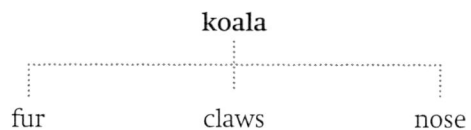

Class to sub-class:

Creature and attributes:

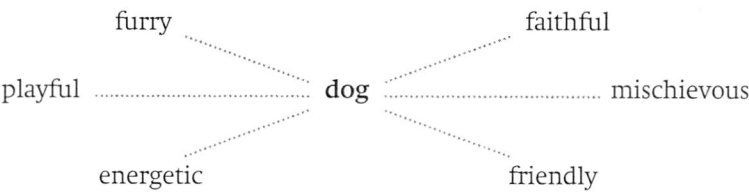

Connectives

Connectives are words or groups of words that link ideas. They can be used between sentences, or to introduce a new paragraph. Connectives give the reader 'signposts', showing how the text is developing and what might come next.

Some examples of connectives are:

Showing time:	now, afterwards
Clarifying:	for example, for instance
Result:	so, therefore, because of this
Keeping ideas in order:	first, to start with
New information:	in addition, furthermore, also
Conditions apply:	however, despite this, besides

REMEMBER

Conjunctions join clauses within sentences.
Connectives form links between sentences, paragraphs and longer pieces of text.

Dialogue patterns

Dialogue patterns refer to different patterns in texts. Texts are held together by dialogue patterns and these are different, according to the *register*.

Register

Register refers to the way a text changes depending on the topic, the people involved and the form of language—whether the text is written or spoken, for instance.

If you feel strongly about a topic, it will change the way you speak about it. You might become more excited, and speak more loudly and more quickly than you would about a topic that you don't really care about.

When you speak, you might use short sentences and few content words. When you write, you will most likely use longer sentences, and more content words.

Below are two different examples of language styles. They are both about the same subject—a car accident—and the same participants are involved. But the register of each example is quite different. One difference in register comes from the fact that the first piece is spoken by the participants, face-to-face, and the second piece is a letter written by one of the drivers.

Notice how the language in Text 1 differs from that of Text 2. In Text 1, the language is informal, and the people speaking are angry and upset. In Text 2, the language is very formal and, although the writer is still angry about the accident, the tone of the letter is quite calm.

TEXT 1

The Accident

First driver:	You ran into the back of me! You hit my car!
Second driver:	Why did you stop so suddenly?
First driver:	I had to brake; there's a sharp corner.
Second driver:	I couldn't stop when you braked like that.
First driver:	It's your fault; you were too close. I'm calling the police!
Second driver:	Call them then; we'll see who's in the wrong.
First driver:	That man over there saw what happened. He can be a witness. He'll back me up. What's your name and address?

TEXT 2

Dear Sir,

I have decided to report yesterday's accident to my insurance company. You will be hearing from them in due course.

The detail of the accident has been explained, particularly regarding the fact that you hit my car from behind and were not travelling at a safe distance.

I regret that the matter was not reported to the police immediately, but I have now informed them of the incident, together with the name of the witness who saw the accident.

Yours,
John Smith

Differences in texts

The following diagram shows how various factors affect difference in a text.

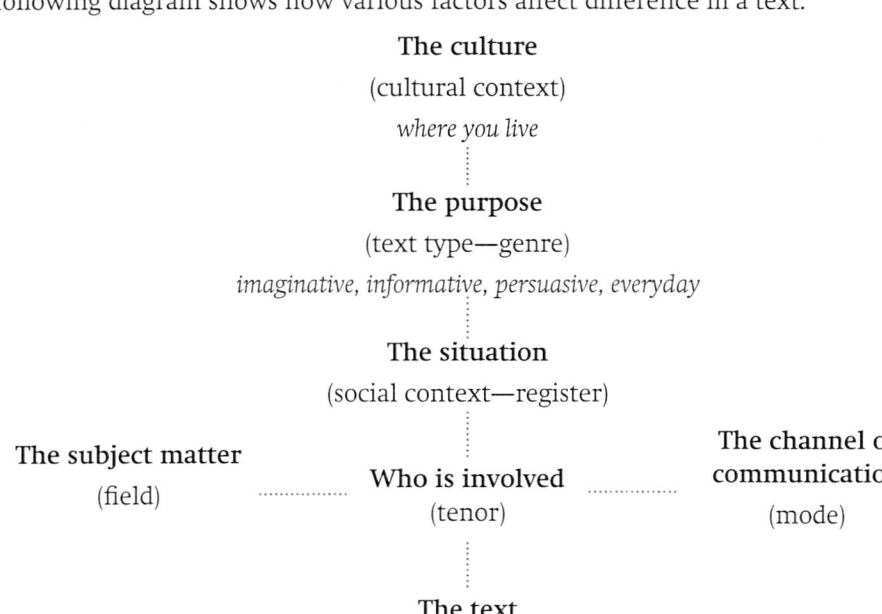

The culture

(cultural context)

where you live

The purpose

(text type—genre)

imaginative, informative, persuasive, everyday

The situation

(social context—register)

The subject matter	Who is involved	The channel of communication
(field)	(tenor)	(mode)

The text

SUBJECT MATTER (Field)	WHO IS INVOLVED (Tenor)	THE FORM OF THE LANGUAGE (Mode)
through	through	through
Participants	**Mood**	**Theme**
Persons, places, things, ideas	Declarative (indicative), interrogative, imperative	(First part of a message) (Prominent, foregrounded)
• Noun groups/phrases	• Statements	• Noun group/phrase
	• Questions	• Verb group/phrase
	• Commands	• Adverb group/phrase
		• Prepositional phrase
Attributes	**Modality**	**Rheme**
(Qualities of participants)	Degree of usuality and probability	(Remainder of sentence)
• Noun groups/phrases	Obligation	
• Adjective groups/ phrases	• Adverb groups	
	• Modal groups (*must, should*)	

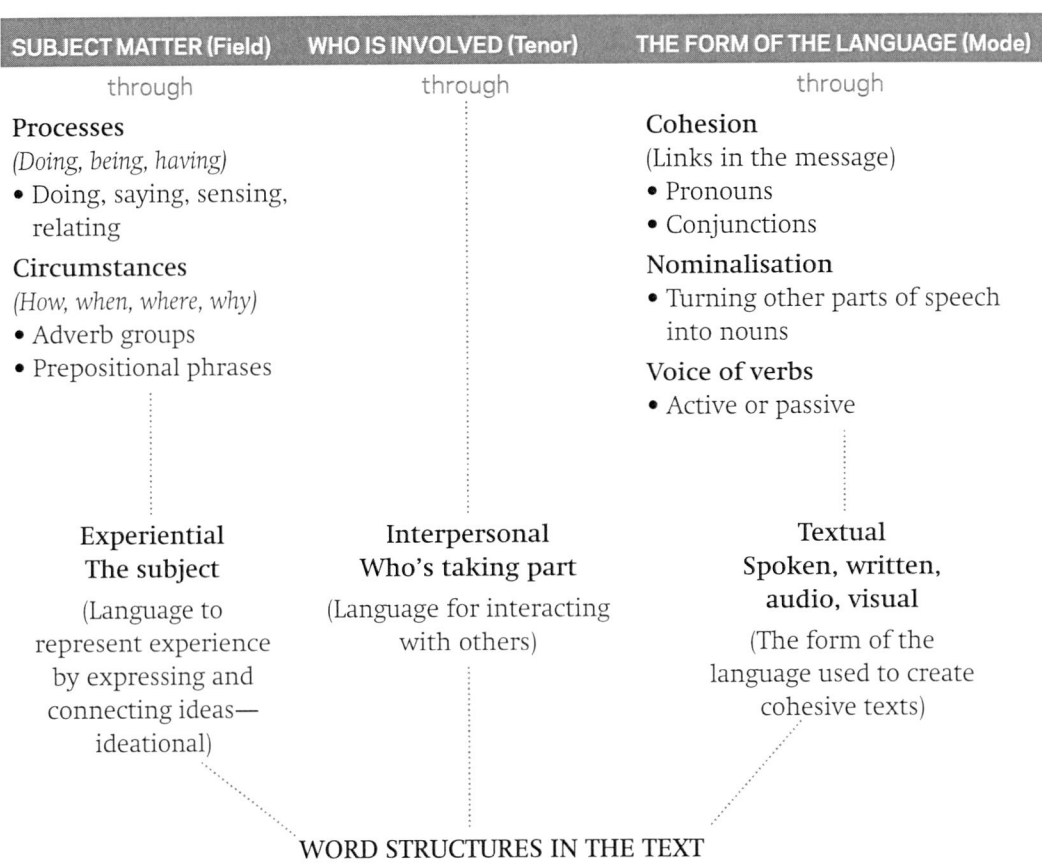

SUBJECT MATTER (Field)	WHO IS INVOLVED (Tenor)	THE FORM OF THE LANGUAGE (Mode)
through	through	through

Processes
(Doing, being, having)
• Doing, saying, sensing, relating

Circumstances
(How, when, where, why)
• Adverb groups
• Prepositional phrases

Cohesion
(Links in the message)
• Pronouns
• Conjunctions

Nominalisation
• Turning other parts of speech into nouns

Voice of verbs
• Active or passive

Experiential
The subject

(Language to represent experience by expressing and connecting ideas— ideational)

Interpersonal
Who's taking part

(Language for interacting with others)

Textual
Spoken, written, audio, visual

(The form of the language used to create cohesive texts)

WORD STRUCTURES IN THE TEXT

Clause structures to represent experience

These consist of:		These can be:
Participants	persons, places, things and ideas	nouns noun groups/phrases pronouns adjectivals
Attributes	describe the participants	adjectivals noun groups
Processes	action/doing, being, saying, sensing (thinking/feeling)	verbs verb groups/phrases
Circumstances	things that surround the event; how, when, where, why	adverbials adverbial clauses

Example

At the airport the passengers talked quietly about the flight. They were very excited.

Circumstance: At the airport

Participants: the passengers

Process: talked

Circumstance:	about the flight.
Participant:	They
Process:	were
Attribute:	very excited.

Language structure of personal interaction

Through sentence types

These consist of:		These can be:
Declarative	statement	mood: indicative
Interrogative	question	mood: interrogative
Imperative	command	mood: imperative
Subjunctive	doubt, possibility, wish	mood: subjunctive

Different grammatical moods are found to be more common in different genres. For example, instructional texts contain verbs in the imperative mood.

Through modality

These consist of:		These can be:
Degrees of usuality	often, sometimes, always, seldom, never	adverbs of time
Degrees of certainty	possibly, probably, maybe	modal adverbs
Degrees of obligation	must, should, ought, will	auxiliary verbs or modals

Language structures for constructing texts

Theme

The theme comes first in a clause, and indicates what the sentence is about. It is the predominant part. The pattern of the themes in a text shows how the text develops. The theme is not necessarily the subject of a sentence.

Rheme

The **rheme** is the remainder of the clause—everything except the theme.

At the airport the passengers talked happily about the flight.

| **Theme:** | At the airport |
| **Rheme:** | the passengers talked happily about the flight. |

Cohesion

Cohesion links ideas in a text.

At the airport the passengers talked happily about the flight.

They were very excited.

In these sentences, the pronoun *they* is linked to the noun *the passengers*.

Types of cohesion

There are a number of different types of cohesion: *reference*, *substitution*, *ellipsis*, *conjunction*, and *related words* (also known as *lexical*).

- *Reference* means using pronouns that refer back or forwards to nouns.

  The **man** was tall. **He** was also thin.

- *Substitution* means using a different word.

  My **dog** is a good **one**.

- *Ellipsis* means leaving out words.

  The man was tall and **[he was]** thin.

- *Conjunction* means using conjunctions or adverbs to link phrases, clauses, sentences and paragraphs.

  The captain **and** the crew came on shore.

  He ran hard; **then** he swerved.

- *Related words* means using words that have similar meanings.

  The man was a thief, a criminal, a villain.

Traditional/modern grammatical terms

Throughout this handbook, we have used a mixture of traditional and modern grammatical terms. The following table sets them out side-by-side, and explains what they mean.

Terms in traditional grammar	Terms in modern grammar	What they mean
Adjective or adjectival phrase	Attribute or adjectival	A word or phrase that adds meaning to a noun.
Adverb or adverbial phrase	Circumstance or adverbial	A word or phrase that adds meaning to a verb, adjective or other adverb.
Auxiliary verb	Auxiliary verb	A part of a verb that makes up the verb group. It shows tense or mood.
Clause	Clause	A group of words with a finite verb.
Conjunction	Conjunction	The linking of ideas in a text.
Connections between different parts of speech, sentences and paragraphs (cohesion)	Cohesion Reference Substitution Ellipsis Conjunction Related words (lexical)	A joining word in a text.
Finite verb	Finite verb	A verb that has a subject.
Inflection	Inflection	A suffix added to a noun or verb to show number or tense.

Terms in traditional grammar	Terms in modern grammar	What they mean
Main idea at beginning of clause	Theme and rheme	The placing of the main idea (theme) at the beginning of a clause for emphasis. The rheme is the remainder of the clause.
Mood Indicative Imperative	Mood and modality Declarative Interrogative Imperative	Verb forms that indicate statements, questions and commands.
Mood Subjunctive	Modality	Doubts, wishes, possibility, probability or certainty expressed through modal auxiliary (traditional) or modals and modifiers (functional).
Noun	Participant Also represented by pronouns and noun groups	The name of a person, place or thing.
Participle	Participle	Part of a verb in a verb group (or verb phrase) or used as an adjective.
Phrase	Phrase	A group of words without a finite verb doing the work of different parts of speech.
Preposition	Preposition	A word that introduces a prepositional phrase.
Principal clause	Independent clause	A clause that has a single, self-contained message; it can stand by itself.
Pronoun	Pronoun	A 'positioning' word that stands instead of a noun. In modern grammar, pronouns can constitute the noun group.
Sentence	Sentence Clause complex	One or more clauses linked together in meaning. One clause must be the principal (independent) clause. Each sentence begins with a capital letter and ends with a full stop, question mark or exclamation mark.
Subject and predicate	Participant and process with an optional circumstance	The subject is the focus of the verb. The predicate contains the finite verb and its modifiers.

Terms in traditional grammar	Terms in modern grammar	What they mean
Subordinate clause	Dependent clause Embedded clause	A clause that is linked to a principal clause. A subordinate clause cannot stand alone.
Tense Present Past Future	Tense Present and timeless present Past Future	The form of the verb that indicates when the action occurs
Verb	Process (Also shown by verb groups including modifiers)	A word in a sentence that states what is happening
Voice Active Passive	Voice Active Passive	In the active voice in traditional grammar, the subject is the doer. In the passive voice, the subject is acted upon. In modern grammar, the doer is the theme and the receiver of the action is in the theme position.

Text types/genres

Text types classify texts according to purpose.

Text types can be divided into two main types: imaginative (literary) and factual. The structure of each text type is determined by the purpose for which the text is written. It is important to remember that there can be overlap between text types, and that texts are not restricted to the printed word.

The following text types are examined:

* Literary/Imaginative Texts: narrative, literary recount, literary description, literary review, poetry.
* Factual Texts: factual description, information report, procedure, factual recount, explanation, persuasion (exposition and discussion).

Literary texts

A literary text is a text that entertains. Literary texts use imaginative, creative elements and language.

Narrative

Social purpose: A narrative tells a story by constructing a pattern of events. The events may have an outcome that the reader or listener finds unexpected or that may raise a problem. A narrative entertains because it stimulates creative thinking, and it instructs because it makes the reader or listener think and feel about the characters and happenings in the story. Examples of narratives are *The Lord of the Rings* by J.R.R. Tolkien, *Charlotte's Web* by E.B. White, and *Watership Down* by Richard Adams.

Narratives can be long or short and may be written in prose or verse. Prose narratives are written in 'everyday', straightforward language. Verse narratives use more figurative, poetic language. Examples of prose narratives are *Harry Potter and the Philosopher's Stone* by J.K. Rowling, and *Little Women* by Louisa May Alcott. Examples of verse narratives are *The Highwayman* by Alfred Noyes, and *The Man from Snowy River* by A.B. Paterson.

Structure: A narrative is usually made up of an orientation, a complication and a resolution, in which the problems are commonly worked out. Sometimes a narrative finishes with a comment by the author. This is called a *coda*.

Grammatical features of a narrative:

* uses particular nouns that refer to or describe the characters or events
* uses adjectives and adjectival phrases and/or clauses that build up a description of the parts of the story
* uses past tense action verbs
* uses *saying*, *thinking* and *feeling* verbs to indicate what a character is feeling, thinking or saying
* uses adverbs and adverbial phrases and/or clauses to locate where or when the action takes place
* uses conjunctions and time connectives to show the sequence of events.

An example of a narrative:

Theseus and the Minotaur

Structure	Text	Some language features
Orientation	The **Minotaur** was a terrifying monster with the head and shoulders of a bull and the body of a man. It lived in the palace of **King Minos** of Crete and ate the flesh of	proper nouns
	humans. King Minos had built a **labyrinth**, or maze, made of stone to keep the	common noun
	Minotaur prisoner. The labyrinth was so **complicated** that no one who entered it had	
	found their way out again.	adjective group/phrase

Complication

King Minos **had thought** up a cruel plan for
feeding the Minotaur. Every year King Minos
made **King Aegeus** of Athens send **seven young**
men and **seven young** women to Crete to be fed to
the Minotaur. Every year this caused much grieving
amongst the people of Athens.

thinking verb

proper noun

adjective groups/ phrases

Series of events

One year, Theseus, the son of King Aegeus,
said he would take the place of one of the young
people and find a way to kill the Minotaur. The King
and Queen and all the other mothers and fathers
sadly waved the young people goodbye as they set
sail for Crete. When the seven men and
seven women arrived on Crete they were
immediately taken to the palace. There, King
Minos's beautiful daughter, Ariadne, saw Theseus
and **instantly** fell in love with him. She decided to
help him kill the monster.

saying verb

adverbs

Ariadne **arranged** to meet Theseus secretly at
the entrance to the labyrinth. When they met she
gave him a sword and a ball of silken thread. 'Be
very careful,' she **warned** him. 'The labyrinth is as
dangerous as the Minotaur.'

past tense action verb

saying verb

Theseus (**who was as clever as he was handsome and brave**), **tied** one end of the thread to a rock at the entrance of the labyrinth. **As he felt his way along the dark tunnels**, he unrolled the thread until eventually he came to a place scattered with skulls and bones. Suddenly, Theseus heard a deafening roar and quickly **turned** around. **Luckily** he dodged the fearsome horns of the Minotaur **just in time. Swiftly**, he swung his sword and with enormous strength struck the horrible beast across the back. Then he stood still and waited and listened. Before long he heard an even louder roar. The Minotaur had only been wounded **by the first blow** and now it attacked **again**. This time Theseus **plunged** his sword straight into the Minotaur's heart. Now there was only silence **in the labyrinth**.

— adjectival clause

— past tense action verb

— adverbial clause

— adverb group/phrase

— past tense action verb

— adverb groups/phrases

— past tense action verb

Resolution

Theseus **recovered** his breath and followed the thread back to the entrance where Ariadne was nervously waiting for him. He took her aboard his ship and they sailed away with the young Athenian men and women he had saved. Theseus became a hero and he and Ariadne **were married with King Aegeus's blessing**.

— past tense action verbs

— adverb group/phrase

Literary recount

Social purpose: A literary recount retells the sequence of events as they happened in a literary context and enables the author to make a judgment about those events and/or the characters. Its purpose is to give an entertaining and personal rendition of events. It may be either oral or written and the narrative may be in the form of prose or verse.

Examples include the retelling of tales of the exploits of mythical heroes such as Jason, Theseus and Hercules. Others are the recounts of the experiences of famous people, like Sir Edmund Hillary's historic climb of Mt Everest, or the exploits of the young man from Snowy River.

Structure: A literary recount is made up of an introduction and a record of events that may contain personal comments by the author. These comments may seek to evaluate or judge events or the behaviour of the characters. This is usually followed by a reorientation that rounds off the text by incorporating comments and attitudes about the events or the characters.

Grammatical features of a literary recount:
* uses nouns and pronouns to identify the characters of the story
* uses adjectives and adjectival phrases and/or adjectival clauses that describe the nouns and pronouns
* uses action verbs that refer to the events
* uses past tense verbs to give a sense of the writer's or storyteller's time
* uses adverbs and adverb groups/phrases and/or adverbial clauses that indicate place and time
* uses conjunctions and connectives to show the sequence the events.

A literary recount has the same structure and common grammatical features as a factual text, whose purpose is to recount events or procedures. (See Factual recount pp. 80–1.)

Literary description

Social purpose: A literary description describes in literary terms a particular thing, such as a place, an animal, a person or something that happened in nature. The emphasis is on individual things, not on a general class of things. A literary description can also be imaginative.

A literary description can be part of a narrative or another literary text. It makes us look closely at a thing to see what it is really like. Examples are: the descriptions of the hobbit's hole at the beginning of *The Hobbit* by J.R.R. Tolkien; the Coorong at the beginning of *Storm Boy* by Colin Thiele; and the animals in *The Wind in the Willows* by Kenneth Grahame.

Structure: A literary description is made up of an introduction and a description, and may end with a personal evaluation by the author. This can take the form of a concluding (ending) comment.

Grammatical features of a literary description:
* uses proper nouns identified from the literary text
* uses detailed noun groups to provide more information about a particular person or thing
* uses adjectives and adjective groups/phrases and/or adjectival clauses that give an opinion; a factual description; an amount or numerical number (quantity); or classify a noun

- uses relating verbs and sensing verbs to give the author's personal viewpoint, and action verbs to describe the characters' behaviour
- uses adverbs and adverb groups/phrases and/or adverbial clauses that provide information about the characters' behaviour
- uses figurative language, such as metaphors, to enhance meaning.

A literary description has the same structure and common language features as a factual description (see p. 77), whose purpose is to focus attention on the characteristic features of a particular thing. Consequently, when you read a literary text, the result can be a powerful and moving experience for you. It could assist understanding by helping you to identify with both the place and the character. Literary observation is the prelude to literary description.

An example of a literary description

Wongadilla

Structure	Text	Some language features
Introduction and descriptive features	Wongadilla is one knot in a tangle of spurs and ridges. You would say it is much like other sheep-runs nearby but Charlie claims it is greener. Its steepest, sharpest height is called 'the mountain' but really it is a clump of high and higher tops melted together in one. There are green places high and low and slopes of tall grass the colour of moonlight; shade trees everywhere, and a patch or two of scrub, and rock breaking through in the steepest places. Halfway down its looming height, the mountain spreads a broad lap, and from there, throws out three ridges into the flat between it and the opposite mountain. One of these is … like a long arm running out from under its rocky shoulder. This ridge is covered in forest and lies half in Wongadilla and half outside it; Charlie's boundary fence, running down	metaphor — proper noun — relating verbs — detailed noun group — adjective group/phrase — simile — detailed noun group

the mountain, cuts across this ridge and through

the forest, and takes in the flat below. The flat

spreads wide between this ridge and the other

two, like the space between your thumb and your

first two fingers.
The other two ridges lie close together, holding

between them a narrow, deep gully where the creek

runs down to the river. Where they join the mountain

is the round green swelling of a hill, and behind this

is a hollow that is always green with a glint. This

is the swamp. When you come to it, hidden on the

side of the mountain and halfway up to the crest of

the wind, then you begin to know Wongadilla.
If you go into the swamp you feel no squish

of mud but rough clean water-couch springing

under your toes. Rafts of pink-tipped weed drift

with the wind, drawing its pattern in lines on the

water. Jelly-froth rafts of frog-spawn are moored to

tufts of bull-grass, for the swamp is always loud with

the creaking and hiccupping of frogs. There are

rootled-out snuffed-up holes where a wombat was

feeding — a tuft of clean mauve fur left by a swamp-

wallaby—it is like seeing a door close as someone

slips away.

adverb group/ phrases

simile

detailed noun group

adjectival clause
relating verb

detailed noun group

action verbs

relating verb

prepositional phrase

relating verb

detailed noun groups

adjectival clause

adverbial clause

Concluding comment

(Patricia Wrightson, from *The Nargun and the Stars*)

Literary review

Social purpose: A literary review is a response to a text. This response may summarise and/or analyse the appeal and value of that text to a reader. A review can be either oral or in written form. Some examples of texts that are reviewed are books, films, exhibitions, musical performances and dramatic presentations of all types. They can be reviewed in newspapers, magazines and other media.

Structure: A literary review can contain information about the author/composer, actors/ performers, characters and the setting. This can be called the *context*, and is followed by a summary of the incidents (*text description*). Finally, the reviewer makes an *evaluative response* (judgment), which indicates what he/she thinks of the text and its appeal to an audience.

A preliminary stage to a literary review is a *personal response*, in which students give spoken responses to a literary text, a film, a piece of art, a building—anything that involves creative composition.

Grammatical features of a literary review:

* uses *relating, action, saying* and *thinking verbs* with noun groups to describe characters
* uses the present tense (which may change to the past tense if the text has a historical setting)
* includes a time sequence of events, because only the key events are summarised
* uses persuasive language when the author is making a judgment
* includes clause or sentence themes that are often the title of the book or of other creative pieces of composition
* includes the name of the author, actors, directors or performers.

An example of a literary review

A Review of Storm Boy

Structure	Text	Some language features
Context	Storm Boy **is** a novel by the Australian author Colin Thiele. It **is** an exciting story about the friendship between a boy and a pelican **that the boy raised from a chick**.	relating verbs in the present tense adjectival clause
Text description	Storm Boy **lives** with his father, Hide-Away Tom, in a humpy in a wild part of South Australia beside the Southern Ocean. The area is also a sanctuary for many species of birds. Storm Boy and his father live an isolated life collecting 'treasures' blown in with the tide, and befriending all living creatures. He is a happy boy who **loves** the wild storms that lash the area.	timeless present tense sensing (feeling/ thinking) verb

The pelican **is raised** by Storm Boy, who calls

····· passive voice

it Mr Percival, **after hunters kill the bird's**

····· adverbial clause

parents and destroy the nest. After rescuing

and raising Mr Percival, Storm Boy **tries**

····· action verb in the present tense

to return him to the bird sanctuary, but the

pelican keeps coming back. They become best

friends and have many adventures together.

Judgment I really **enjoyed** the book, particularly the

····· sensing (feeling) verb

descriptions of Ninety Mile Beach and the

animals that live there. The words paint

····· adverb group/phrase

pictures in your mind. **It is an easy book to**

read because it is not very long and the

····· complex sentences

interesting story makes you want to read to

find out what happens next. The ending

is a little bit sad but it is also hopeful.

····· compound sentence

I would recommend this book for primary

school students.

Poetry

Social purpose: Poetry is written to achieve a wide range of social purposes. Poetry expresses feelings and reflections on experience, people and events. It is primarily an *aesthetic* (beautiful or artistic) experience that works mainly through emotions, sensory experience and imaginative perceptions. It may concentrate on the feelings and reflections of the poet, or it may tell a story. It describes people, places or things in poetic ways that makes it distinguishable from prose, especially by creating images in striking ways through techniques such as *simile, metaphor, alliteration, assonance* and *onomatopoeia*.

Sound qualities in the form of rhyme and rhythm are an important component of poetry. However, the main purpose is to give enjoyment through an understanding of the literary and language devices that are used to concentrate and enhance meaning.

Structure: Poetry is often written in 'chunks' or stanzas. The form that a stanza takes may involve a structure, like the *ode* or *haiku*, or it may be free-formed. Literary devices are used to enhance meaning, and words are used that compress meaning so that a poem uses the best possible words in the best possible order.

There are many recognised types or forms of poems. Here are some, listed in alphabetical order: acrostic poem, ballad, catalogue poem, cinquain, concrete poem, Dylan Thomas portrait, epic, Ezra Pound couplet, free verse, haiku, limerick, lyric, ode, sonnet.

Grammatical features of poetry

These vary enormously depending on the social purpose of the poem, but most rely on features of textural cohesion such as *word chains* based on devices like *repetition, synonym* and *antonym*. Story poems use features of story texts such as action verbs, noun groups, adverb groups/phrases and adverbial clauses, and adjective groups/phrases.

An example of a poem

Sort of Brown

Most things **aren't** any real colour — being verb

in my **town**; — rhyme

they're sort of **brown**, — figurative language (simile)

like dust and dead leaves

and **sleeves** — figurative language (alliteration) — rhyme

that had been on people

for a day or **two**. — word chain (cohesion)

Most things aren't **red or green**

or yellow or **blue**; — rhyme

they're sort of brown

I **think**. — thinking verb

Don't **you**? — repetition (cohesion)

Gordon Winch

Factual texts

A factual text provides information.

Factual description

Social purpose: Factual description focuses our attention on the features of a particular thing. It may relate to a person and may contain some personal comment by the author; it may be an impression of a particular event; or it may be a description that depends on the careful and thorough detailing of time and events.

Structure: A factual description is made up of an introduction to the subject, followed by a description of the characteristic features of that subject, and may conclude with a comment by the author. It has the same structure as a literary description but differs from it because the resulting factual description is based on direct observation rather than on the observation and description made by someone else.

The common grammatical features are the same as those involved in *literary description.* (See p. 72.)

Information report

Social purpose: An information report gives factual information about a class of things.

Structure: An information report is made up of a general statement about the subject, including information that may define and classify that subject, followed by a description that may contain a comment about its importance. (See Factual description, above.)

Grammatical features of an information report:

- uses general nouns
- uses relating verbs to describe features
- uses action verbs to describe behaviour
- uses the timeless present tense of verbs to indicate 'usualness'
- uses technical terms
- uses paragraphs with a topic sentence that organises information
- repeats the name of the topic or generalised subject of the text as the beginning focus of the clause.

An example of an information report

Sharks

Structure	Text	Some language features
General statement about a class of things	Sharks **are** among the largest, deadliest	relating verbs
	and most feared **creatures** in the sea.	general noun
	Yet most **are** harmless and many make	cohesive tie
	excellent eating.	
Facts	Sharks **have been** in the oceans for	relating verb
	350 million years. They are survivors	
	because they are bold and active	
	animals. There are at least 350 different	
	species of sharks, which can be divided	
	into two groups: the sharks **with**	adjective group/ phrase
	cigar-shaped bodies, and the rays,	

which have flattened bodies. ◄·················· adjectival (clause)

Facts   Sharks and rays have no bones. Their

timeless present tense

skeletons **are made** from **cartilage**.

technical nouns

You can feel cartilage at the tip of your

nose or the top of your ears.

Facts   Sharks have their mouths below their

snouts. **Also, they** have five to seven

cohesive tie

gill slits on either side of their heads.

Note: Repeated naming of the topic—sharks

Fish only have one gill on either side.

Procedure

Social purpose: A procedure tells us how to do or make something. Recipes, rules of games, instructions that explain how to grow things and how to go from place to place are examples of procedures.

Structure: A procedure is made up of a goal for the activity; a list of any skills, equipment and materials needed to achieve that goal; and finally the steps or instructions that show you what to do. These may be numbered.

Grammatical features of a procedure:

* uses commands
* uses action verbs in the present tense
* uses precise vocabulary
* uses adverbs and adverb groups/phrases and clauses that express details of time, place and manner.

A **procedural recount** is the retelling or rewriting of a set of procedures that have been formulated by someone else. They may not reflect personal experience. Telling how a famous chef cooks a particular dish can be a procedural recount.

An example of a procedure

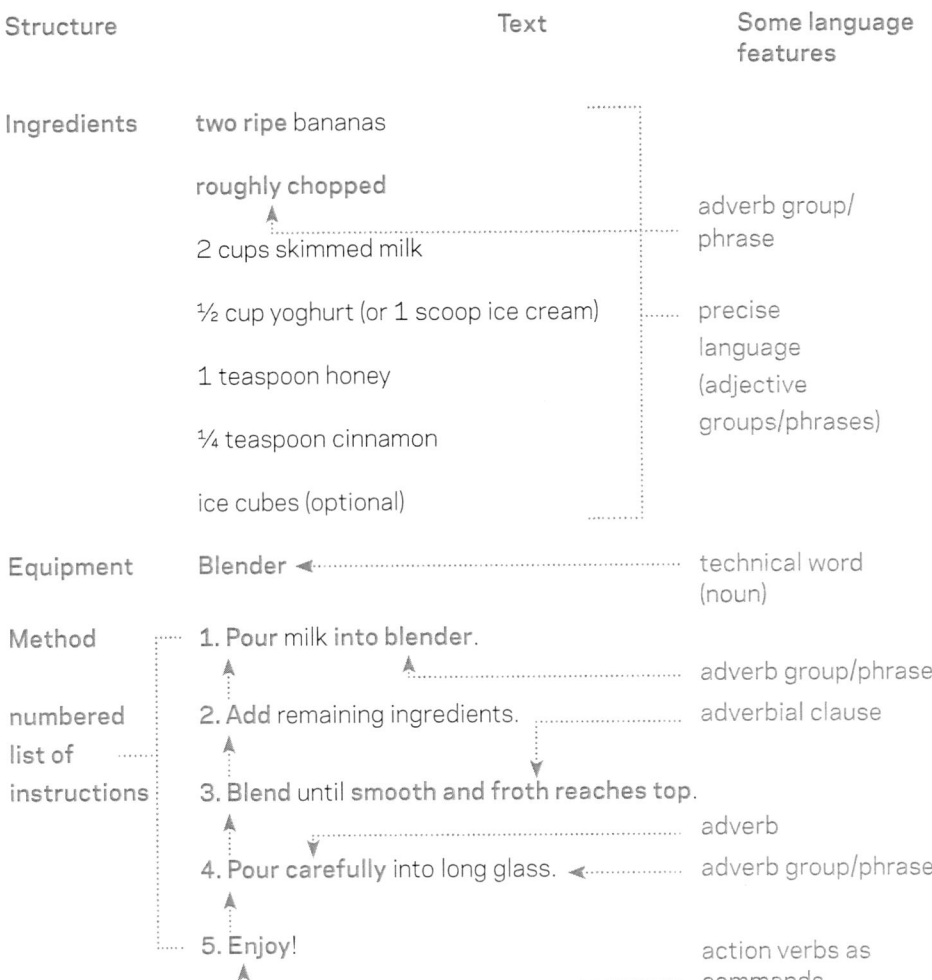

How to Make a Banana Smoothie

Structure	Text	Some language features
Ingredients	two ripe bananas	
	roughly chopped	adverb group/phrase
	2 cups skimmed milk	
	½ cup yoghurt (or 1 scoop ice cream)	precise language (adjective groups/phrases)
	1 teaspoon honey	
	¼ teaspoon cinnamon	
	ice cubes (optional)	
Equipment	Blender	technical word (noun)
Method	1. Pour milk into blender.	adverb group/phrase
numbered list of instructions	2. Add remaining ingredients.	adverbial clause
	3. Blend until smooth and froth reaches top.	adverb
	4. Pour carefully into long glass.	adverb group/phrase
	5. Enjoy!	action verbs as commands

Factual recount

Social purpose: A factual recount documents a series of events and attempts to evaluate their significance in some way. Accounts of holidays, school visits and sporting events are all factual recounts.

Structure: A factual recount begins with an orientation that gives information about the people and the events in the recount (*who, when, where* and *why*), followed by a record of events in the order in which they occurred. Personal comments, which may include making a judgment, are often interspersed throughout the record of events. The text concludes with a reorientation that rounds off the sequence of events.

Grammatical features of a factual recount:

- uses nouns and pronouns to identify characters or events
- uses adjectives or adjective groups/phrases and clauses to describe these subjects
- uses action verbs to refer to events
- uses past tense verbs to locate events in relation to the speaker's or writer's time

- uses adverbs or adverb groups/phrases and clauses to indicate place and time
- uses conjunctions and connectives to sequence the events.

An example of a factual recount

Our Excursion to Manly

Structure	Text	Some language features
Orientation	Last Wednesday, our class went on an excursion to Manly beach.	adverb groups/ phrases to show time and place
Record of events	We left school **at about nine o'clock** and walked down to the station. **We** caught the train and got off at Circular Quay. **We** were just **in time** for the ferry.	pronouns to signify group
Events	**On the trip over to Manly, we** had to cross the Heads. Here the sea **was** very rough and the waves **crashed** over the bow of the ferry. Some kids were a bit afraid.	relating verb action verb pronoun to signify group
Events	**We** arrived at Manly and **walked** across to the ocean beach where we had our lunch. Our teacher, Mr Downard, **told** us many interesting things about Manly and how it got its name.	action verb saying verb pronoun to signify group
Events	At about two o'clock **we** went back to the wharf to catch the ferry for the trip home. It was still rough crossing the Heads.	Note: The beginning of each paragraph gives the sequence of events.

Explanation

Social purpose: An explanation tells how something works or why it occurs in the way it does. Explanations are usually found in scientific and technical fields.

Structure: An explanation begins with an introduction that states what is to be explained, followed by a series of steps in the explanation. It may conclude with a final statement that sums up. Explanations may include diagrams, illustrations, charts and/or tables.

Grammatical features of an explanation:

- uses abstract nouns
- uses noun groups for greater precision
- uses technical language
- uses action verbs in the simple present tense
- uses the passive voice
- uses adverbs or adverb groups/phrases and clauses, especially using conjunctions of time (when) and cause (why)
- uses compound sentences extending meaning.

An example of an explanation

How the Telephone Works

Structure	Text	Some language features
Introduction	A telephone works like the human ear.	noun group
	The vibrations of the speaker's vocal	technical language (noun)
	chords produce air vibrations which	
	make the listener's eardrums vibrate.	technical language
	These vibrations are magnified and	
	our hearing nerves carry the sound	abstract noun
	message to our brain.	
Explanation	Telephones allow this process to take	common noun
	place over distances where speech	adjectival (clause)
	wouldn't carry.	technical language (nouns)
Explanation	A telephone has a handpiece. In the	
	handpiece there is a transmitter and	
	a receiver. The transmitter contains	
		relating verbs

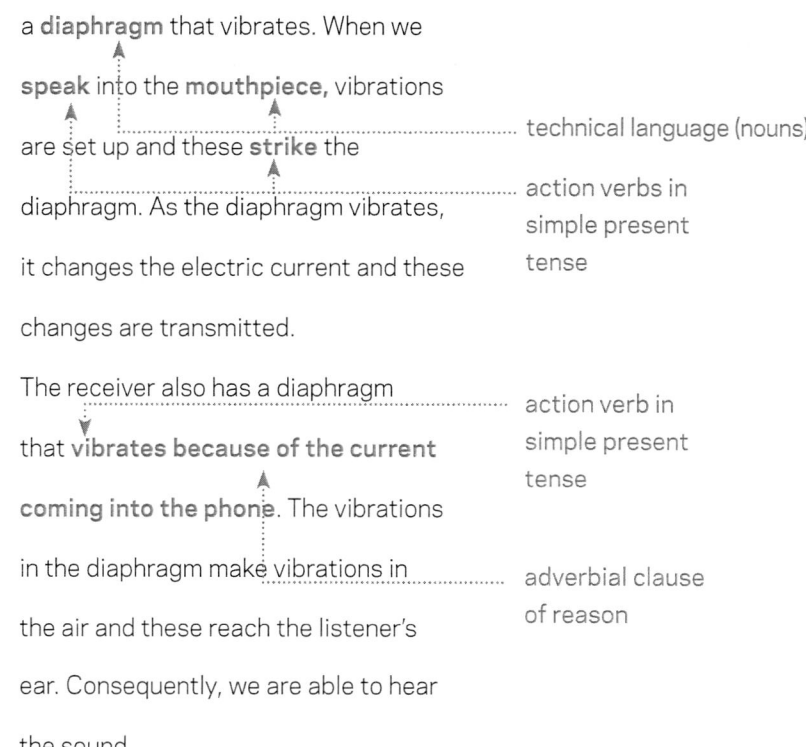

a **diaphragm** that vibrates. When we

speak into the **mouthpiece,** vibrations .... technical language (nouns)

are set up and these **strike** the .... action verbs in simple present tense

diaphragm. As the diaphragm vibrates,

it changes the electric current and these

changes are transmitted.

Explanation   The receiver also has a diaphragm .... action verb in simple present tense

that **vibrates because of the current**

coming into the phone. The vibrations

in the diaphragm make vibrations in .... adverbial clause of reason

the air and these reach the listener's

ear. Consequently, we are able to hear

the sound.

Persuasive texts

Persuasive texts present an argument. They attempt to persuade, or convince, the reader to agree with a particular point of view.

Exposition and *discussion* are types of persuasive texts.

Exposition

Social purpose: An exposition argues a case for or against a point of view or belief. Its purpose is to argue a case and to persuade someone to agree with the argument.

Structure: An exposition is made up of an opening statement that describes the position taken. This is followed by a statement supporting that position. This statement must be supported with evidence. The first statement made is usually the strongest argument supported with the most compelling evidence. The order in which 'point and elaboration' are arranged depends on the author. Finally, there will be a concluding statement that restates the opening position more forcefully in the light of the evidence presented.

Grammatical features of an exposition:
* uses general and abstract nouns and will probably contain technical words
* uses evaluative adjectives that give weight to the nouns and reinforce the author's commitment to the argument
* uses relating, action and thinking verbs
* uses modal verbs and adverbs to reinforce the author's commitment to a position
* uses connectives to give order and structure to the evidence-supported position.

The most common form of oral exposition is the *debate*, where teams argue for or against a stated position. It is the role of the affirmative side to make the case for the given proposition. The negative side makes the case against it. Both sides must use evidence to support their arguments.

An example of an exposition

Ban Cars from Our Cities!

Structure	Text	Some language features
Introduction	Cars **should** be banned from our major cities. Our cities **are** heavily polluted and cars are one of the main causes of this. Cars **are** also **dangerous** and **noisy**.	modal verb — relating verbs — adjectives
Argument	Cars contribute a lot to the pollution of our cities. Cars' exhaust gases are deadly to humans. These gases cause lung diseases like **asthma** and **bronchitis**. Many people end up in hospital because of these **diseases**.	technical nouns — common noun
Argument	**Secondly**, many people live and work in our cities. Cities are busy places with pedestrians clogging narrow footpaths or rushing across busy streets. Cars make such crossings very dangerous. **Pedestrians** are **knocked** over and sometimes **killed** by careless motorists.	connective — common noun — action verbs

	Everyone **knows** that cars are the	sensing (thinking) verb
	biggest killers on our roads.	
Argument	**Lastly**, cars are very noisy. During the	connective
	day this noise distracts workers. Noise	
	can also make telephone conversations	
	difficult. At night city residents find	adjective
	it very hard to sleep **because of the**	
	traffic noise. Sometimes when you are	adverb group/ phrase
	at the pictures you can hear the traffic	
	noise. This **can** spoil your enjoyment of	modal verbs
	the movie.	
Concluding statement reinforcing position	Our cities **would be** healthier, **much** safer and **less** noisy places if cars were	
	banned from the streets.	modal adverbs

Discussion

Social purpose: A discussion presents both sides of an argument. It enables us to hear, read and write different points of view about a subject.

Structure: A discussion is made up of a statement that outlines an issue, and is often accompanied by some background information about that issue. Arguments for and against the proposition should include supporting evidence. A discussion, which involves weighing up the arguments, should conclude this text. This might sum up both sides of the argument or it may include a recommendation in favour of one side. Each side tries to persuade the audience.

Grammatical features of a discussion:

* uses general nouns
* uses detailed noun groups to provide information in a compact way
* uses relating verbs to provide information about the issue
* uses thinking verbs to express the author's personal view
* uses adverbs or adverbial phrases/clauses of manner
* uses modal adverbs to express degree
* uses additive, contrastive and causal connectives to link arguments.

An example of a discussion

Work and Play—Which Is More Important?

Structure	Text	Some language features
Introduction statement	Which is the more important part of our lives—work or play? **Work** is doing something because it will bring a benefit. Play is doing something for its own sake because we like doing it. **Play** is what we do when we are not working or doing things like sleeping, washing ourselves or eating.	common nouns
Arguments for and against	Most of the **activities** that we do at school are work. Through **schoolwork** we learn many useful things. I **think** reading, writing, maths and all the other subjects are important. They give us skills that we can use throughout our lives. I also **believe** it is important to learn and work hard to gain the **skills** necessary for a good job later in life. We work at home too. We work at	sensing (thinking) verb
		sensing (thinking) verb
		common noun

home because we are part of a family

and work helps both the family and us.

On the other hand, **imagine** our **lives** if ············· common noun

all we did was work. How boring would ············· sensing (thinking) verb

that be? You **might** have heard this old ············· modal verb

saying: '*All work and no play makes Jack*

a dull boy.'

Play is anything we do because we enjoy it. ············· common noun

It **might** be a game, or going to the ············· modal verb

beach, or seeing a movie, or just playing

with your dog. **However**, I believe play

can also teach us many things. It can

teach us how to work together and be ············· connectives

a member of a group. **For example**,

playing in a team makes us think of

someone other than ourselves. Play

often involves doing physical things, ············· modal adverb

so play also has an important part in

keeping us fit and well. ◄············· adverbial clause of reason

Conclusion

In conclusion, we need both work and

play in our lives. We learn from both

and both **can** be enjoyable. **In addition**,

both work and play **can** help us to be

mentally and physically fit. **The most**

important thing in life is to get the

balance between work and play

just right.

Sometimes this is harder than you think!

connectives

modal verbs

detailed noun group

Correct usage

Confused words

Many words in the English language are often used incorrectly, either because they sound or look similar to another word with a different meaning, or because they have a similar meaning.

Here is a list of words that are often confused. They are arranged in alphabetical order for easy reference.

The confused-word pairs in this list are entered once only. If you look for a word and cannot find it, try looking for another word with which it is likely to be confused. For example, the word *uninterested* does not have a separate entry, but you will find it under the entry *disinterested • uninterested*.

Each entry will tell you about the words and why they are different. Using the correct word helps you communicate your meaning more clearly.

accept • except

accept	A verb meaning 'to receive something'. They **accept** small gifts from his church.
except	A subordinate conjunction or preposition meaning 'not including'. Links clauses or phrases. He would have won **except** he pulled a muscle. They all went **except** me.

acute • chronic

acute	An adjective meaning 'very sudden and severe'. Mum had an **acute** vomiting attack.
chronic	An adjective meaning 'occurring over a long time'. He has a **chronic** ear problem.

AD • BC

AD	The abbreviation of *Anno Domini (in the year of our Lord)*. It refers to the years after the birth of Christ. James Cook came to Australia in **AD** 1770.
BC	The abbreviation of *before Christ*. It refers to any years before AD 1. The Romans came to Britain in 55 **BC**.

advice • advise

advice	A noun meaning 'a recommendation someone gives you'. I was given good **advice** by my teacher.
advise	A verb meaning 'to give someone a recommendation'. I **advise** you to use your dictionary.

affect • effect

affect	A verb meaning 'to cause a change'. I hope the change will not **affect** you too much.
effect	A noun meaning 'the result'. The win had a great **effect** on the team.

a lot • many/much

a lot	An adjective used with amounts of things. There was **a lot** of water in the boat.
many	An adjective used with objects you can count. There were **many** chairs in the room.
much	An adjective used with amounts of things that can't be counted. There was too **much** air in the tyres.

all ready • already

all ready	A phrase meaning 'prepared'. When we were **all ready**, we jumped in the car.
already	An adverb meaning 'earlier' or 'beforehand'. I have **already** told you I won't go to the game.

a.m. • p.m.

a.m.	The time from midnight to noon. We have breakfast at 8 **a.m.**
p.m.	The time from noon to midnight. Afternoon tea is served at 3 **p.m.**

ante- • anti-

ante-	A prefix meaning 'before'. My mum is going to an **ante**natal clinic at the hospital.
anti-	A prefix meaning 'against' or 'opposed to'. My dad took part in the **anti**-war demonstrations.

anxious • eager

anxious	An adjective meaning 'to be nervous'. She was very **anxious** waiting for the train to arrive.
eager	An adjective meaning 'keenly wanting'. She was **eager** to do well in her exams.

anybody • anyone

	Singular pronouns that take a singular verb. **Anybody knows** that six plus four is ten.

anything • anythink

anything	A pronoun meaning 'any thing'. **Anything** could happen in this match.
anythink	A non-word that should never be used.

as • like

as	A subordinate conjunction that can begin a clause. I reached for the handle **as** the light went out.
like	A preposition that can begin a phrase. He plays football **like** his skilful brothers.

assure • ensure • insure

assure	A verb meaning 'to make confident'. I **assure** you that your dog will be well cared for.
ensure	A verb meaning 'to make certain'. Will you **ensure** that you will be here tomorrow?
insure	A verb meaning 'to buy insurance'. We will **insure** our house for $200,000.

astrology • astronomy

astrology	A noun meaning 'the study of the supposed effects of the planets and stars on the lives of humans'. Madam Startreck used **astrology** to tell me that next Friday would be an exciting day for me!
astronomy	A noun meaning 'the study of the universe'. A telescope helps us in our study of **astronomy**.

aural • oral

aural	An adjective concerning the ear and hearing. Her **aural** test proved she needed a hearing aid.
oral	An adjective concerning the mouth and talking. The **oral** test was harder than the written examination.

bath • bathe

bath	A noun meaning 'a place where we wash our bodies' or 'the act of washing in a bath'. There is a **bath**, a shower and a toilet in the bathroom. I'm going to have a **bath** before tea.
bath	A verb meaning 'to wash with water'. I **bath** the baby in a plastic tub.
bathe	A verb meaning 'to clean something with water' or 'to swim'. Tom's dad **bathed** his grazed leg. The family **bathed** at Noosa Beach.

began • begun

began	The past tense of the verb 'to begin'. He **began** swimming when he was five.
begun	The past participle of the verb 'to begin'. He has **begun** lessons with a new coach.

beside • besides

beside	A preposition meaning 'next to'. They sat **beside** the lake.
besides	A preposition meaning 'apart from'. No one else will be there **besides** John.

biannual • biennial

biannual	An adjective describing something that happens twice a year. The group had its **biannual** meetings in April and September.
biennial	An adjective describing something that occurs every two years. The next **biennial** meeting will be held in two years.

both • each

both	Refers to two people or things. Always takes a plural verb. **Both** Jim and Jane **are** coming.
each	Refers to people or things individually. When used before the noun/pronoun, it always takes a singular verb. **Each** has a good chance of winning the race. When **each** is used after the noun/pronoun, it takes a plural verb. They **each have** a good chance of winning.

bought • brought

bought	The past tense and past participle of the verb 'to buy'. We **bought** a new jumper for my young brother.

brought	The past tense and past participle of the verb 'to bring'. We **brought** our new baby brother home.

breath • breathe

breath	A noun meaning 'the air going in or out of the lungs'. He took a deep **breath** before the dive.
breathe	A verb meaning 'to make air go in or out of the lungs'. Humans cannot **breathe** underwater.

broke • broken

broke	The past tense of the verb 'to break'. He **broke** the record last Wednesday.
broken	The past participle of the verb 'to break'. He has **broken** seven records this year.

can • may

can	A helping verb meaning 'to be able to do something'. I **can** climb that tall tree.
may	A helping verb meaning 'to be allowed to do something' or 'might do something but it isn't certain'. **May** I come to your birthday party? They **may** arrive soon.

cardinal numbers • ordinal numbers

cardinal numbers	A compound noun meaning any ordinary numbers. There are **30** children in my class.
ordinal numbers	A compound noun that shows place in a series. Friday will be the **21st** day of the month.

cloth • clothe

cloth	A noun meaning 'a piece of woven material'. The suit was made from woollen **cloth**.
clothe	A verb meaning 'to put on clothes'. For the play, I will **clothe** her in old rags.

compare • contrast

compare	A verb used for things that are alike. **Compare** this apple to this pear.
contrast	A verb used for things that do not share common qualities. The blue curtains **contrast** with that bright yellow wall.

complement • compliment

complement	A verb meaning 'to make something complete'. The dessert will **complement** your meal.
compliment	A verb meaning 'to praise'; a noun meaning 'a word of praise'. I want to **compliment** your team on its performance. I gave the team a **compliment**.

continual • continuous

continual	An adjective describing something that happens again and again usually with short breaks in between. The team's **continual** complaints drove the coach mad.
continuous	An adjective describing something that goes on without a break. The **continuous** noise from the car alarm kept me awake.

could have • could of

could have	A verb phrase. ✓ James **could have** been the school captain this year. ✗ James ~~could of~~ been the school captain this year.
could of	Is used mistakenly because of the confusion of the contraction of 'have' ('ve) with 'of'. The same applies to 'should have' and 'would have'.

dairy • diary

dairy	A noun or adjective meaning 'a place where cows are milked'. Mr Holloway used to own a **dairy** at Berry. [noun] His **dairy** cows were all Illawarra Shorthorns. [adjective]
diary	A noun or adjective meaning 'a book with a day-to-day record of events'. I keep my **diary** in a secret place. He makes a **diary** entry for every telephone call.

device • devise

device	A noun meaning 'a tool or simple machine'. Penny invented a **device** for sharpening pencils.
devise	A verb meaning 'to make, invent or work out'. Bruce will probably **devise** a plan for staying away from school.

did • done

did	The past tense of the verb 'to do'. He **did** his homework every night.
done	The past participle of the verb 'to do'. He has **done** all his homework.

different from/than/to

different from	This is the accepted form of this expression, although modern usage now accepts 'different to' in spoken form. My watch is **different from** my teacher's.
different than/ different to	These are not used in written language. ✓ He is **different from** me. ✗ He is ~~different to~~ me. ✗ He is ~~different than~~ me.

disinterested • uninterested

disinterested	An adjective meaning 'impartial' or 'unbiased'. He was a **disinterested** observer at the conference.
uninterested	An adjective meaning 'not interested'. William is very **uninterested** in biology.

drove • driven

drove	The past tense of the verb 'to drive'. He **drove** his father's car too fast.
driven	The past participle of the verb 'to drive'. He has **driven** from Brisbane today.

either ... or • neither ... nor

either	This is always linked with 'or' and takes a singular verb. **Either** Jim **or** Pete has won the race.
neither	This is always linked with 'nor' and takes a singular verb. **Neither** the team **nor** its coach was happy.

elder/eldest • older/oldest

elder/eldest	Adjectives describing age relationships within a family. John is the **elder** brother. Phillip is the **eldest** child in that family.
older/oldest	Adjectives meaning 'more old' or 'most old'. That elephant is **older** than its keeper. That horse is the **oldest** one in the stable.

emigrate • immigrate

emigrate	A verb meaning 'to leave your home country'. Many people decided to **emigrate** from Italy after the war.
immigrate	A verb meaning 'to arrive and live in a new country'. Many Italian, Greek and Turkish families **immigrated** to Australia. You emigrate **from** somewhere. You immigrate **to** somewhere.

employee • employer

employee	A noun meaning 'a person who is employed'. James White is an **employee** of a bank.
employer	A noun meaning 'a person or company who employs another person'. Wise **employers** treat their workers well.

everybody • nobody • somebody

	These are pronouns used in relation to a group of persons; they take a singular verb.
everybody	**Everybody** has a chance to win.
nobody	**Nobody** is available to play.
somebody	**Somebody** is responsible. Modern usage now allows us to use the plural pronoun 'they' with these pronouns. **Everybody** says that **they** should be at school.

everyone • no one • someone

	These are pronouns used in relation to individual persons who make up a group; they take a singular verb.
everyone	**Everyone** is guilty.
no one	**No one** is free to go.
someone	**Someone** has to pay!

everything • nothing • something

	These are pronouns used in relation to things; they take a singular verb.
everything	**Everything** is provided.
nothing	**Nothing** is given away.
something	**Something** is happening.

explicit • implicit

explicit	An adjective meaning 'clearly defined, stated or set down'. He gave an **explicit** recount of the events.
implicit	An adjective meaning 'not clearly defined or stated but implied or suggested'. The team has an **implicit** understanding of how the game should be played.

export • import

export	A noun or verb to do with sending goods out of a place. Australia would like to **export** more products. [verb] Our largest **export** is coal. [noun]
import	A noun or verb to do with bringing goods into a place. Australia **imports** many foreign-made cars. [verb] Our largest **import** is probably foreign cars. [noun]

farther • further

Either is correct; further is generally preferred.
The **further** they went, the **further** he dropped behind.
The superlative of further is **furthest**.

few • couple

few	An adjective meaning 'more than two things'. John played a **few** games of football.
couple	An adjective meaning 'two things'. I had a **couple** of slices of toast for breakfast.

fewer • less

fewer	An adjective that refers to things that can be counted. There are **fewer** boys than girls in our class.
less	An adjective that refers to something that can't be counted but can be measured. There is **less** water in the dam than there was last year.

final • finale

final	A noun meaning 'the last of a series'; can also be an adjective. Our team made the **final** last year. [noun] Is that your **final** offer? [adjective]
finale	A noun meaning 'the last part of a performance'. The orchestra played the **finale** with great style.

flaunt • flout

flaunt	A verb meaning 'to put something on show to make others envious'. I bet she will **flaunt** her new skateboard at the park!
flout	A verb meaning 'to ignore a rule on purpose'. Oliver has been known to **flout** the school rules.

formally • formerly

formally	An adverb derived from the word 'formal' meaning 'to do something in a formal way'. He dressed **formally** for the event.
formerly	An adverb derived from the word 'former' meaning 'something done before'. He was **formerly** a teacher but is now a writer.

former • latter

These are pronouns when they work together and refer to people, places and things that have already been mentioned.
Former is the first of two and latter is the last of two.
Bach and Chopin are famous composers; the **former** was German and the **latter** was Polish.

former	An adjective meaning 'previous'. He is the **former** principal of the school.

from • off

from	A preposition. I bought it **from** that shop.
off	An adverb. The wheels fell **off**. **From** and **off** are often confused when writing about exchanging things. You buy or take **from** a person. ✓ I bought my bike **from** James. ✗ I bought my bike ~~off~~ James.

gave • given

gave	The past tense of the verb 'to give'. He **gave** all his money to charity.
given	The past participle of the verb 'to give'. He has **given** her a beautiful book.

gone • went

gone	The past participle of the verb 'to go'. I had **gone** to the movies.
went	The past tense of the verb 'to go'. I **went** to school even though I was sick.

good • well

good	An adjective or adverb. She is a **good** netball player. [adjective] The team looked **good**. [adverb]
well	An adverb. They played that match **well**. There is a difference in meaning between **good** and **well** in the following expressions: Tom is looking **well**. [healthy] Tom is looking **good**. [doing something well or looking attractive] Using 'good' in this way is colloquial but now generally accepted.

hanged • hung

hanged	The past form of the verb 'to hang' but refers specifically to a method of execution. Ned Kelly was **hanged** at the Old Melbourne Gaol.
hung	The past form of the verb 'to hang' but refers to a thing rather than a person. They **hung** the meat in the coolroom.

have • of

	Have and of are sometimes confused because **have** is contracted to -ve in such phrases as **could have** (could've), **should have** (should've) and **would have** (would've). **Have** is always a verb. **Of** is a preposition and never a verb. ✓ The team should **have** won that match. ✗ The team should ~~of~~ won that match.

honorary • honourable

honorary	An adjective describing something done for no pay. He is the **honorary** treasurer of our club.

honourable	An adjective describing a person who does good things. She is a very kind and **honourable** person. The term 'honourable' is used formally in the title of members of parliament. The **Honourable** Julia Gillard, MP, is Australia's first female prime minister.

hyper- • hypo-

hyper-	A prefix meaning 'too much'. She was a **hyperactive** child.
hypo-	A prefix meaning 'under' or 'too little'. He was given an injection with a **hypodermic** needle.

inter- • intra-

inter-	A prefix meaning 'between' or 'among'. The cars crashed at the **intersection**.
intra-	A prefix meaning 'within' or 'inside'. When you fly from Sydney to Wagga, you are travelling on an **intrastate** route.

laid • lain

laid	The past form of the verb 'to lay'. You always lay something somewhere. He **laid** the plates on the table.
lain	The past form of the verb 'to lie'. You lie or rest somewhere with your body. After you have **lain** down, you will feel much better.

lay • lie

lay	A verb meaning 'to put down'. It always requires an object. You lay something somewhere. He **lays** his hand on the table.
lie	A verb meaning 'to be or rest in a flat position'. Every summer, Mum tells me not to **lie** in the sun.

learn • teach

learn	A verb meaning 'to acquire knowledge or information'. He will **learn** to play the piano when he is seven.
teach	A verb meaning 'to pass on knowledge or information to instruct others'. Will you **teach** me how to make a chocolate cake?

lend • loan

lend	A verb meaning 'to give something temporarily'. I **lend** money to my friends.
loan	A noun meaning 'money or objects you give to someone temporarily'. ✓ Don gave me a **loan** of five dollars. ✗ Don gave me a ~~lend~~ of five dollars.

lightning • lightening

lightning	A noun meaning 'a discharge of electricity in the atmosphere'. The **lightning** flashed and the thunder roared.
lightening	The present participle of the verb 'to lighten', meaning 'to reduce the weight of something'. **Lightening** the load in my schoolbag made it easier to carry.

loose • lose

loose	An adjective meaning 'not tightened or fixed'. The **loose** nut caused the accident.
lose	A verb meaning 'to mislay'. Did you **lose** your front-door key?

loud • loudly

loud	An adjective describing a high volume of noise. There was a **loud** bang.
loudly	An adverb that should never be used as an adjective. ✓ The band played **loudly**. ✗ The band played ~~loud~~.

me • my

me	A personal pronoun, first person, objective case. He gave the ball to **me**.
my	A possessive or pronominal adjective. ✓ It's **my** ball. ✗ It's ~~me~~ ball.

of • off

of	A preposition indicating distance or direction; contents; belongings or possessions. Wollongong is south **of** Sydney. A kilogram **of** potatoes. He is a friend **of** mine.
off	A preposition, adverb or adjective meaning 'away from' or 'no longer a part of'. He slipped and fell **off** the ladder. [preposition] The wheels fell **off**. [adverb]

persecute • prosecute

persecute	A verb meaning 'to act against a person or group in an unjust, cruel way'. Jews were **persecuted** during the Second World War.
prosecute	A verb meaning 'to take legal action against'. Mr Jones was **prosecuted** for dumping rubbish in the street.

precede • proceed

precede	A verb meaning 'to go before'. His fame **preceded** him.
proceed	A verb meaning 'to go forward'. He **proceeded** along the street at a brisk pace.

prescribe • proscribe

prescribe	A verb meaning 'to order treatment'. The doctor **prescribed** antibiotics to treat the infection.
proscribe	A verb meaning 'to forbid'. The teacher **proscribed** talking in class.

purposefully • purposely

purposefully	An adverb meaning 'to do something with enthusiasm and determination'. He **purposefully** worked at the portrait of his friend.
purposely	An adverb meaning 'to do something intentionally'. He **purposely** avoided seeing his sister.

raise • rise

raise	A verb meaning 'to lift up'. The past form is 'raised'. He **raised** the banner above his head.
rise	A verb meaning 'to get up or go upwards'. The past forms are 'rose' and 'risen'. The balloon **rose** above the earth. Note that **raise** takes an object, but **rise** does not.

ran • run

ran	The past tense of the verb 'to run'. He **ran** in three races.
run	The past participle of the verb 'to run'. He has **run** in three races.

rang • rung

rang	The past tense of the verb 'to ring'. The bell **rang** at 3.20 p.m.
rung	The past participle of the verb 'to ring'. The bell has **rung** three times this afternoon.

real • really

real	An adjective meaning 'genuine'. He is a **real** friend.
really	An adverb meaning 'truly'. ✓ The weather was **really** foul. ✗ The weather was ~~real~~ foul.

receipt • recipe

receipt	A noun meaning 'a document recording that something has been paid for'. I paid the money and was given a **receipt**.
recipe	A noun meaning 'a list of ingredients and instructions'. Here is the **recipe** for a rich chocolate cake.

reserve • reverse

reserve	A verb meaning 'to keep something for a special purpose'. He **reserved** his seat on the express train.
reverse	A verb meaning 'to go backwards'. She **reversed** the car out into the street.

respectable • respectful

respectable	An adjective meaning 'having the respect of others'. She was a **respectable** lawyer.
respectful	An adjective meaning 'showing respect for others'. The whole town was **respectful** of the work Doctor Smith was doing.

rhyme • rhythm

rhyme	A noun and a verb. Words with a similar ending-sound, like 'boy' and 'toy', rhyme. Some people prefer poems that rhyme.
rhythm	A noun meaning the beat of music or verse. The music had a strong Latin rhythm.

ridden • rode

ridden	The past participle of the verb 'to ride'. Have you ever ridden a horse?
rode	The past tense of the verb 'to ride'. I rode a horse in Centennial Park last week.

sang • sung

sang	The past tense of the verb 'to sing'. She sang three songs at the concert.
sung	The past participle of the verb 'to sing'. ✓ She has already sung four verses. ✗ She has already sang four verses.

saw • seen

saw	The past tense of the verb 'to see'. ✓ I saw the accident. ✗ I seen the accident.
seen	The past participle of the verb 'to see'. I have seen several accidents at this corner.

sewage • sewerage

sewage	A noun meaning 'the waste matter that goes into the sewer'. Raw sewage is sometimes allowed to flow into the sea.
sewerage	An adjective that describes the system of sewage-removal. The sewerage system in Sydney is very old.

shall • will

shall	An auxiliary verb showing future tense. Used in the first person, or in the second and third person to show emphasis. I shall be going on holiday next Monday. You shall be on time! [emphasis]
will	An auxiliary verb showing future tense. Used in the second and third person, and in the first person to show emphasis. They will be going on holiday next Monday. I will be there! [emphasis]

so • that

so	An adverb used to intensify meaning and used like 'very'. ✓ I was so tired I couldn't stay awake. ✗ I was that tired I couldn't stay awake.
that	Should never be used as an adverb!

sometime • sometimes

sometime	An adverb describing an indefinite point in time. Sometime soon we will be going on holiday.

sometimes	An adverb meaning 'on some occasions'. My English uncle visits us **sometimes**. When **some time** is part of a phrase, it is written as two words. I will be at school for **some time** to come.

stalactite • stalagmite

stalactite	A noun meaning 'a column of rock formed by dripping water'. **Stalactites** grow down from the roof.
stalagmite	A column of rock formed by dripping water. **Stalagmites** grow up from the floor. (Remember: The 't' in stalactite stands for 'top', so a stalactite grows down from the top. The 'g' in stalagmite stands for 'ground' so a stalagmite grows up from the ground.) There are both **stalactites** and **stalagmites** in the Jenolan Caves.

stole • stolen

stole	The past tense of the verb 'to steal'. The thief **stole** Mum's diamond ring.
stolen	The past participle of the verb 'to steal'. My bike has been **stolen**.

subconscious • unconscious

subconscious	An adjective meaning 'just below conscious level'. Something in his **subconscious** told him not to do it.
unconscious	An adjective meaning 'not conscious'. He was knocked **unconscious** by a cricket ball.

sympathy for • sympathy with

sympathy for	This means 'to feel sorry for someone'. I have great **sympathy for** farmers who are fighting the drought.
sympathy with	This means 'to be in agreement with an idea'. I have **sympathy with** the idea that schoolchildren should have less homework.

that/those • this/these

that/those	Demonstrative pronouns or demonstrative adjectives that refer to things that are not close by. **That** boat over there seems out of control. **Those** birds are being a nuisance to those picnickers.
this/these	Demonstrative pronouns or demonstrative adjectives that refer to things that are nearby or close to **This** book is very old. **These** books are very old.

them • they

them	Personal pronoun, third person, plural, objective case. I gave **them** away.
they	Personal pronoun, third person, plural, nominative case. ✓ **They** are all in one family. ✗ ~~**Them**~~ are all in one family.

them • those

them	Personal pronoun, third person, plural, objective case. I gave flowers to **them**.
those	Demonstrative pronoun or demonstrative adjective. ✓ **Those** books belong to the library. ✗ ~~Them~~ books belong to the library.

translucent • transparent

translucent	An adjective meaning 'lets in light but can't be seen through'. Coloured window blinds are **translucent**.
transparent	An adjective meaning 'able to be seen through'. I use **transparent** plastic to wrap my lunch.

try and • try to

try to	A verb form that is usually followed by an infinitive. **Try to** finish your homework before tea. This is preferred to writing 'try and'. ✓ **Try to** eat your vegetables. ✗ ~~Try and~~ eat your vegetables.

unless • without

unless	A subordinate conjunction meaning 'except on the condition that'. I won't go **unless** you go too.
without	A preposition meaning 'not accompanied by, not using or not having'. I won't go **without** you.

what • which

	What and which can be used as interrogative pronouns or interrogative adjectives. **Which** book is it in? **What** book is it in? **Which** can also be a relative pronoun while **what** can never be. ✓ This is the book, **which** I borrowed from the library. ✗ This is the book ~~what~~ I borrowed from the library.

Homonyms

The word *homonym* means 'the same name'. There are different kinds of homonyms, such as homophones and homographs. They are all homonyms.

Homophones
Homophone means 'the same sound'. Homophones are words that have the same sound but are spelled differently and have different meanings.

creak   creek   dear   deer   heard   herd

Homographs
Homograph means 'the same writing'. Homographs are words that have the same spelling, but have different meanings.

grate: part of a fireplace

grate: to rub into small parts, as in *to grate cheese*

desert: a place with very little rainfall

desert: to leave or run away

Some words are both homophones and homographs.

bow: the front end of a boat

bow: to bend over

Below is a useful list of homonyms. There are many more, but these are some of the most common.

allowed • aloud

allowed	The past tense and past participle of the verb 'to allow'. I **allowed** them to come in.
aloud	An adverb meaning 'to speak audibly or to cry out'. He cried **aloud** with pain.

band • banned

band	A noun meaning 'a company or crowd', often of musicians. The **band** played 'Waltzing Matilda'.
band	A noun meaning 'a strip of material used to bind things together'. The papers were held with a rubber **band**.
banned	Past tense of the verb 'to ban', meaning 'to forbid'. They **banned** him for seven matches.

bare • bear

bare	An adjective meaning 'uncovered'. I had **bare** feet.
bear	A noun—a type of animal. A polar **bear** is white.
bear	A verb meaning 'to carry, hold up or put up with'. I will **bear** the weight. I cannot **bear** the pain.

base • bass

base	A noun meaning 'the bottom part of a thing'. The **base** of the cliff.
base	A noun meaning 'headquarters'. army **base**
bass	A noun meaning 'the lowest musical pitch'.

be • bee

be	A verb meaning 'to exist'. I will **be** home at eight o'clock.
bee	A noun—a type of insect. The **bee** buzzed around on the bottlebrush flowers.

bean • been

bean	A noun—an edible vegetable. The **bean** is green.
been	The past participle of the verb 'to be'. I have **been** to see him.

berry • bury

berry	A noun—a small fruit. I ate a red **berry**.
bury	A verb meaning 'to cover in the ground'. My dog likes to **bury** his bone.

berth • birth

berth	A noun meaning 'a place where you sleep in a boat or train'; or 'a place where a ship ties up at a dock'.
berth	A verb meaning 'to tie up at a wharf or dock'. The ship **berthed** at Dock 14.
birth	A noun meaning 'the process of being born'. We celebrated the **birth** of the baby.

bight • bite • byte

bight	A noun meaning 'an indentation in the coastline'. The Great Australian **Bight**.
bite	A noun and a verb meaning 'to grab with your teeth'. A big **bite** of pie. [noun] To **bite** a piece of pie. [verb]
byte	A noun meaning 'a unit of information stored by a computer'.

blew • blue

blew	The past tense of the verb 'to blow'. I **blew** the trumpet.
blue	An adjective and a noun—the name of a colour. a **blue** sweater [adjective] **Blue** is my favourite colour. [noun] You can also feel blue when you are unhappy.

board • bored

board	A noun meaning 'a flat piece of wood'; the name of a group of people who are in charge of an activity; or a verb meaning 'to pay to live at a place'. The **board** of the company met monthly.
bored	The past tense of the verb 'to bore' meaning 'to make a hole'. The machine **bored** a hole. Bored can also mean 'uninterested'. The movie **bored** them.

boarder • border

boarder	A noun meaning 'someone who pays to live at a place'.
border	A noun meaning 'the edge or side of a thing'.
border	A verb meaning 'to form the edge of a thing'. The new property will **border** our place.

bough • bow

Both words rhyme with cow.

bough	A noun meaning 'the limb of a tree'.
bow	A noun meaning 'the front of a boat'.
bow	A verb meaning 'to bend over'. Can also be a noun. The actor will **bow** to the audience. [verb] She took a **bow**. [noun]

bow • bow

Both words rhyme with so.

bow	A noun—a knot with two loops. I wear a **bow** tie.

bow	A noun meaning 'a device used to fire an arrow'. a **bow** and arrow
bow	A noun—a special stick used to play a violin.

boy • buoy

boy	A noun—a male child.
buoy	A noun—a marker in the water.
buoy	A verb meaning 'to support'. to **buoy** someone up

brake • break

brake	A noun—something that slows a machine.
brake	A verb meaning 'to slow or stop'. **Brake** as you come to the corner.
break	A noun—a gap; an attempt to escape; a short rest.
break	A verb meaning 'to fracture something'. Don't **break** the glass.

bread • bred

bread	A noun—a type of food made from flour, water and yeast. I like eating fresh **bread** and butter.
bred	Past tense of the verb 'to breed', meaning 'to produce young'. He **bred** cattle on his farm.

buy • by • bye

buy	A verb meaning 'to purchase something'. Can also be a noun meaning 'something that is bought'. What did you **buy**? [verb] a good **buy** [noun]
by	An adverb meaning 'near' or 'past something'. They went **by**.
by	A preposition meaning 'near to'. I sat **by** the pool.
bye	A noun—a run in cricket when the batsman does not hit the ball; or when a competitor doesn't have to play in a particular round of a contest. We had a **bye**.
bye	A shortened form of 'goodbye'.

caught • court

caught	The past tense of the verb 'to catch'.
court	A noun—a place where games are played; where royalty and their helpers live; or where legal cases are heard.
court	A verb meaning 'to try to win someone's love or favour'. The prince will **court** the princess.

cell • sell

cell	A noun—a small room in a prison; a tiny part of all living things; a part of a battery; or a computer term.
sell	A verb meaning 'to give a thing to someone in exchange for payment'. Would you like to **sell** that bike?

cent • sent • scent

cent	A noun—one hundredth of a dollar.
sent	The past tense and past participle of the verb 'to send'. I **sent** you a postcard. You have **sent** me a postcard.
scent	A noun—a pleasant smell; a perfume.
scent	A verb meaning 'to smell'. The dogs **scented** the fox.

cereal • serial

cereal	A noun—a type of grain; or a type of breakfast food.
serial	A noun—a film, play or story that continues episode by episode.

check • cheque

check	A verb meaning 'to stop or prevent'; or 'to see if something is correct'. to **check** their progress **Check** your answers.
check	A noun meaning 'something that stops your progress'; or a term used in chess. You are in **check**. [in a game of chess]
check	An adjective—a pattern made up of squares. a **check** skirt
cheque	A noun meaning 'a written order provided by a bank'. I will pay by **cheque**.

choral • coral

choral	An adjective describing something sung by a choir. a **choral** performance
coral	A noun meaning 'the hard, colourful shapes formed from the skeletons of small sea creatures'. a **coral** reef

chord • cord

chord	A noun—a musical term meaning 'three or more notes played together'. I learned a new **chord** on the guitar.
cord	A noun meaning 'something used to tie things together'. a pyjama **cord**

cite • sight • site

cite	A verb meaning 'to quote a book or author'. She was able to **cite** many examples to support her argument.
sight	A noun—meaning 'the ability to see'. My uncle has lost his **sight**.
site	A noun meaning 'a place occupied by a specific subject'. This block of land is the **site** of my new house.
site	A verb meaning 'to locate or place'. It is hoped to **site** the house on this level area.

coarse • course

coarse	An adjective meaning 'thick or rough'; or 'rude or offensive'. **coarse** fabric **coarse** language

course	A noun that has many meanings: golf **course** soup for the first **course** a **course** of lessons The ship's **course** was north.
course	An adverb in the phrase 'of **course**' meaning 'certainly'.

council • counsel

council	A noun meaning 'a group of men and women who make decisions as a group'. My dad works for the local **council**.
counsel	A noun meaning 'advice given after much careful thought'. My grandfather gave me wise **counsel**.
counsel	A verb meaning 'to advise and recommend'. The teacher **counselled** the students to study hard.

creak • creek

creak	A noun meaning 'a squeaky sound'; or a verb meaning 'to make a squeaky sound'. The door **creaked**.
creek	A noun meaning 'a small stream'.

currant • current

currant	A noun—a type of dried fruit.
current	A noun meaning 'a flow of water, electricity or air'.
current	An adjective meaning 'belonging to the present; happening at this moment'. I bought the **current** issue of my favourite magazine.

days • daze

days	A noun—the plural of day. the **days** of the week
daze	A verb meaning 'to stun, confuse or bewilder'. Can also be a noun. He was **dazed** by the blow. [verb] He was in a **daze**. [noun]

dear • deer

dear	An adjective meaning 'greatly loved'; 'costing too much'; or 'respected'. my **dear** friend a very **dear** cut of meat **Dear** Sir or Madam
deer	A noun—a type of animal.

desert • dessert

desert	A noun (say *dez*-urt) meaning 'a dry place'.
desert	An adjective describing a dry place. A **desert** region. [adjective]
desert	A verb (say *de*-zert) meaning 'to run away from or leave something'. Do not **desert** your post.
dessert	A noun (say *de*-zert) sweets at the end of a meal. We had apple pie for **dessert**.

dew • due

dew	A noun meaning 'small drops of water on the grass'.
due	An adjective meaning 'ready to arrive' or 'expected'. The train is **due** soon.

die • dye

die	A verb meaning 'to stop living'.
dye	A noun meaning 'a substance used to change the colour of something'. The **dye** was dark red.
dye	A verb meaning 'to change the colour of something'. Will you **dye** your old coat?

draw • drawer

draw	A verb meaning 'to make a picture with a pen or pencil'.
draw	A noun meaning 'a game that ends with both sides having equal scores'.
drawer	A noun meaning 'a box that slides in and out of a desk or cupboard'. A chest of **drawers**.

ewe • yew • you

ewe	A noun meaning 'a female sheep'.
yew	A noun meaning 'a type of tree'.
you	A pronoun, second person singular or plural personal. **You** are my friend.

fair • fare

fair	An adjective meaning 'light in colour'. **fair** hair It can also mean 'honest' or 'just'. **fair** play It is also a noun meaning 'a group of shows and entertainments set up for a short time'. We went to the town **fair**.
fare	A noun—the money you pay on a train, bus or ferry. a three dollar **fare** It can also mean 'food and drink'. My grandfather likes to eat plain **fare**.

fate • fete

fate	A noun meaning 'the cause of things beyond your control'. It was **fate** that brought us together.
fete	A noun meaning 'a fair where people raise money'. The school **fete** was fun!

father • farther

father	A noun meaning 'a male parent'.
farther	An adverb referring to a greater distance. I ran **farther** than my **father**.

feat • feet

feat	A noun meaning 'a deed of great skill, courage or strength'.
feet	A noun—the plural of 'foot'.

find • fined

find	A verb meaning 'to locate'. He couldn't **find** his hat.
fined	Past tense of the verb 'to fine' someone meaning 'to punish by ordering someone to pay money'. He was **fined** $100 for a traffic offence.

flour • flower

flour	A noun—a type of powder made from crushed grain. Wholemeal **flour** makes delicious bread.
flower	A noun meaning 'the blossom of a plant'; or a verb meaning 'to burst into flower'.

for • fore • four

for	A preposition. I sent **for** my servant.
fore	A noun meaning 'towards the front'. That actor always pushes himself to the **fore**.
four	A noun—the number 4; or an adjective describing the number of things. I ate **four** strawberries. [adjective]

foul • fowl

foul	An adjective meaning 'nasty, dirty, unpleasant'. a **foul** taste
foul	A verb meaning 'to catch or jam'. to **foul** the propeller of a boat
foul	A noun meaning 'a breach of a rule in sport'. That's a **foul**!
fowl	A noun meaning 'a bird kept for eating or for its eggs'.

grate • great

grate	A noun—part of a fireplace; or a screen made by a framework of bars. There was a little **grate** near the bottom of the door.
grate	A verb meaning 'to make into smaller portions by rasping or rubbing against a rough surface'. Thomas liked to **grate** carrots.
great	An adjective meaning 'big, large, important'; or 'very good'. They had a **great** time at the picnic.

groan • grown

groan	A noun meaning 'a sound expressing pain or dismay'; or a verb meaning 'to make a sound expressing pain or dismay'. I **groaned** at Dad's bad joke. [verb]
grown	The past participle of the verb 'to grow'; can also be an adjective. I have **grown** two centimetres. [past participle] a **grown** man [adjective]

hall • haul

hall	A noun meaning 'a corridor, passage or large room'. assembly **hall**
haul	A noun meaning 'an amount taken at one time'. a **haul** of fish
haul	A verb meaning 'to pull hard'. She **hauled** the fish out of the sea.

heal • heel • he'll

heal	A verb meaning 'to make well or cure'.
heel	A noun meaning 'the back part of your foot'.
heel	A verb meaning 'to follow close behind someone'.
he'll	The contracted form of 'he will'.

hear • here

hear	A verb You **hear** with your ear.
here	An adverb of place Come **here**!

heard • herd

heard	The past tense and past participle of the verb 'to hear'. I **heard** you.
herd	A noun meaning 'a large group of animals'. I saw a **herd** of cows.

higher • hire

higher	An adjective or adverb meaning 'more high'. a **higher** jump [adjective] He jumped **higher**. [adverb] Both are comparative degree.
hire	A verb meaning 'to pay money to use or employ'. to **hire** a boat

him • hymn

him	A personal pronoun, third person singular number, objective case. I saw **him**.
hymn	A noun—a type of religious song.

hoarse • horse

hoarse	An adjective meaning 'rough or croaky'. He has a **hoarse** voice.
horse	A noun—a type of four-legged animal.

hole • whole

hole	A noun meaning 'an opening in something'.
whole	An adjective meaning 'all of a thing'. He ate the **whole** cake.

holy • wholly

holy	An adjective meaning 'sacred or religious'. a **holy** person
wholly	An adverb of degree meaning 'completely'. He was **wholly** covered by the water.

hour • our

hour	A noun meaning 'a unit of time'; 60 minutes. I waited for a whole **hour**.
our	A possessive adjective **Our** book is on the table.

in • inn

in	A preposition, or an adverb. He was **in** the pool. [preposition] Come **in**. [adverb]
in	An adjective meaning 'fashionable'. Skinny jeans are **in** this year.

inn	A noun—a type of hotel. They pulled up at the **inn**.

its • it's

its	A possessive adjective or possessive pronoun. **Its** feathers were grey. **Its** does not have an apostrophe when used this way.
it's	A contraction meaning 'it is'. The apostrophe is needed to show that a letter has been left out. **It's** raining today.

key • quay

key	A noun meaning 'something that opens a lock'.
quay	A noun meaning 'a wharf where ships load and unload'.

knew • new

knew	The past tense of the verb 'to know'.
new	An adjective describing something that has just arrived or has just been bought or made.

knight • night

knight	A noun—a nobleman who served the king in medieval times; a person who has been knighted and is called Sir; or a chess piece.
night	A noun—the time of darkness between sunset and sunrise.

knot • not

knot	A noun meaning 'a tangled piece of string or rope, etc'; or a verb meaning 'to tie a knot'. **Knot** the rope so it will not slip.
not	A negative adverb I will **not** do it.

know • no

know	A verb meaning 'to understand'. I **know** where he's hiding.
no	The opposite of yes; not any. He had **no** shoes to wear.

lead • led

lead	A noun (rhymes with head)—a heavy, grey metal. It was as heavy as **lead**.
lead	A verb (rhymes with feed) meaning 'to go in front'. You **lead** and I'll follow.
led	The past tense and past participle of the verb 'to lead' (rhymes with head). He **led** the team onto the field.

loan • lone

loan	A noun meaning 'something you give for a short time'. I gave him a **loan**.
lone	An adjective meaning 'not with anyone or anything'. I sat beneath the **lone** tree.

made • maid

made	The past tense and past participle of the verb 'to make'. They **made** a kite.
maid	A noun meaning 'an unmarried woman'; or 'a female servant'.

mail • male

mail	A noun, verb or adjective relating to letters sent by post. I waited for the **mail** to come. [noun] I will **mail** the letter. [verb] **mail** delivery [adjective]
male	A noun or adjective relating to the opposite of female; men, boys, etc. The **male** lyrebird has a beautiful tail.

main • mane

main	An adjective meaning 'the biggest or most important'. The **main** road is very long.
mane	A noun meaning 'the long hair on the neck of an animal'. The lion tossed its **mane**.

mare • mayor

mare	A noun—a female horse.
mayor	A noun—the head of a city.

meat • meet

meat	A noun meaning 'the flesh of an animal'.
meet	A verb meaning 'to come face to face with someone'.

medal • meddle

medal	A noun—a badge or cross given as a prize or reward.
meddle	A verb meaning 'to interfere'. Don't **meddle** in my affairs.

meter • metre

meter	A noun—a device that measures things. water **meter** parking **meter**
metre	A noun—a measurement of length. This stick is one **metre** long.

miner • minor

miner	A noun—a person who mines. It is also a type of bird.
minor	An adjective meaning 'smaller in size or importance'. The actor had a **minor** part.
minor	A noun meaning 'someone who is not an adult'.

minute • minute

minute	A noun (say *min*-uht)—a unit of time lasting 60 seconds.
minute	An adjective (say muy-*nyooht*) meaning 'very tiny'. The dustmite is a **minute** creature.

missed • mist

missed	The past tense or past participle of the verb 'to miss'. I **missed** the bus. [past tense]

	I have **missed** the bus. [past partciple]
mist	A noun meaning 'a cloud-like vapour, like a fog'.

morn • mourn

morn	A noun—a short form of 'morning'.
mourn	A verb meaning 'to feel sad about someone's death'.

naval • navel

naval	An adjective meaning 'to do with the navy'. a **naval** uniform
navel	A noun—the small hollow in the middle of your stomach. It is where you were attached to your mother before you were born.

oar • or • ore

oar	A noun meaning 'a long stick with a flat end'. You row a boat with **oars**.
or	A conjunction expressing choice. oranges **or** lemons
ore	A noun meaning 'a rock that contains valuable metal'.

one • won

one	A noun—the number 1.
one	An adjective to do with the number 1. I ate **one** apple.
won	The past tense or past participle of the verb 'to win'. I **won** the race. [past tense] I have **won** a trip to Tahiti. [past participle]

pain • pane

pain	A noun meaning 'the feeling you have if you are injured or sick'. I have a **pain** in my foot.
pain	A verb meaning 'to cause hurt or suffering'. It **pains** me to leave you.
pane	A noun—a sheet of glass in a window. They broke a window **pane**.

pair • pare • pear

pair	A noun meaning 'two things that go together'.
pare	A verb meaning 'to cut back or trim away'.
pear	A noun—a type of fruit.

passed • past

passed	The past tense or past participle of the verb 'to pass'. He **passed** everyone in the race. [past tense] I have **passed** my examination. [past participle]
past	A noun, adjective, adverb or preposition. A long time ago, in the distant **past** … [noun] His **past** achievements are amazing. [adjective] He went **past**. [adverb] I walked **past** the window. [preposition]

patience • patients

patience	A noun meaning 'the ability to wait without complaining'.
patients	A noun—the plural of patient, someone being treated medically. The doctor's waiting room was full of **patients**.

paw • poor • pore • pour

paw	A noun meaning 'the foot of an animal with nails or claws'.
poor	An adjective meaning 'having little money'. a **poor** person
poor	A noun meaning 'poor people as a group'. The **poor** need assistance.
pore	A noun meaning 'a tiny opening in the skin'.
pore	A verb meaning 'to study something carefully'. to **pore** over a book
pour	A verb meaning 'to make something flow'. I will **pour** the milk.

peace • piece

peace	A noun meaning 'an absence of war or quietness'. 'Give me a bit of **peace**,' said Mum.
piece	A noun—a part of something. a **piece** of pie It can also mean 'a single thing'. a **piece** of fruit
piece	A verb meaning 'to fit together'. The boy **pieced** a jigsaw together.

plain • plane

plain	A noun—a large, flat area of land. a **grassy** plain
plain	An adjective meaning 'clear and simple'; or 'not beautiful'. a **plain** statement a **plain** face
plane	A noun—the shortened form of 'aeroplane'. the **plane** to Melbourne
plane	A verb meaning 'to make smooth'. He **planed** the timber.

practice • practise

practice	A noun (the 'c' in practice always tells you it is a noun) meaning 'a thing you do over and over'; or 'the usual way of doing something'. I went to football **practice**.
practise	A verb (the 's' in practise always tells you that it is a verb) meaning 'to do something over and over'. I will **practise** my tennis.

principal • principle

principal	A noun meaning 'the head of a school or other institution'; or an adjective meaning 'the main person or thing'. the **principal** actor on the stage
principle	A noun meaning 'a rule or something you believe is right'. He had the highest **principles**.

rain • reign • rein

rain	A noun meaning 'water from the sky'; or a verb meaning 'to fall from the sky in drops'. It **rained** all day.
reign	A verb meaning 'to rule like a king or queen'.
rein	A noun meaning 'a leather strap used to guide or drive a horse'. He held the **reins** in his hand.

rap • wrap

rap	A noun meaning 'a sharp, short knock'; or a verb meaning 'to make a sharp, short knock'. I **rapped** on the door.
rap	An adjective describing a form of dancing and music. I enjoy **rap** dancing.
wrap	A verb meaning 'to cover'. I will **wrap** the present.
wrap	A noun meaning 'a covering'.

raw • roar

raw	An adjective meaning 'not cooked'; or 'not trained'. **raw** meat **raw** recruit
roar	A noun meaning 'a loud, deep sound'; or a verb meaning 'to make a loud, deep sound'. A lion's **roar** is loud! [noun] The lion **roared**. [verb]

read • red

Both words rhyme with bed.

read	The past tense and past participle of the verb 'to read'. I **read** the book yesterday.
red	A noun or adjective—the name of the colour. The girl had **red** hair.

read • reed

Both words rhyme with need.

read	A verb meaning to 'understand the printed word'. He could **read** at the age of six.
reed	A noun—a type of plant that lives in water. He pulled a **reed** out of the creek.

real • reel

real	An adjective meaning 'the genuine thing'. a **real** life story
reel	A noun—something you wind things onto; or a type of dance.
reel	A verb meaning 'to wind in'; 'to stagger or sway'.

right • rite • write

right	An adjective meaning 'correct'. You are **right**. Good work!
right	An adverb or adjective meaning 'the opposite of left'.

	Turn **right** at the next corner. [adverb] I couldn't find my **right** shoe. [adjective]
right	A noun meaning 'a fair claim'. You have a **right** to enter.
rite	A noun meaning 'a ceremony, usually religious'.
write	A verb meaning 'to make letters or words with a pen, pencil or other device'.

ring • wring

ring	A noun—anything shaped like a circular band. a key **ring**; a circus **ring**; a boxing **ring**
wring	A verb meaning 'to squeeze'. I **wring** out the washing when it is wet.

road • rode • rowed

road	A noun—a type of track for people to travel along.
rode	The past tense of the verb 'to ride'. I **rode** the horse yesterday.
rowed	The past tense of the verb 'to row'. We **rowed** in the regatta.

root • route

root	A noun—the part of a plant that grows in the soil.
route	A noun—the way or road you take to go from one place to another. This is the bus **route**.

row • row

row	A noun (rhymes with 'so')—a line of things. A **row** of birds sat on the fence.
row	A verb (rhymes with 'so') I like to **row** a boat.
row	A noun (rhymes with cow)—a noisy quarrel.

sail • sale

sail	A noun meaning 'a sheet that catches the wind on a boat'.
sail	A verb meaning 'to move over water, usually in a boat'. I **sail** every Saturday.
sale	A noun or adjective to do with selling. The **sale** of our house was a lot of work. [noun] I asked the assistant for the **sale** price. [adjective]

sauce • source

sauce	A noun—the tasty liquid you pour on a pie.
source	A noun—the place where something starts. The **source** of the river is in the mountains.

saw • soar • sore

saw	A noun meaning 'a tool with sharp teeth'; or a verb describing what you do with a saw. I will **saw** the wood.
saw	The past tense of the verb 'to see'. I **saw** the movie.

soar	A verb meaning 'to fly upwards or float in the sky'. to **soar** like an eagle
sore	An adjective or noun to do with pain. She has a **sore** foot. [adjective] She has a **sore** on her leg. [noun]

scene • seen

scene	A noun—the place in which the action of a story takes place; or a portion of a play or movie. The **scene** was a darkened dungeon. The actor performed well in the first **scene**.
seen	Past participle of the verb 'to see'. Have you **seen** the way I dance?

sea • see

sea	A noun—a large stretch of water.
see	A verb describing what your eyes do.

seam • seem

seam	A noun—the place where two pieces of cloth are joined.
seem	A verb meaning 'to appear to be'. They **seem** happy.

seas • sees • seize

seas	A noun—the plural of 'sea'.
sees	A verb—part of the verb 'to see'. He **sees** the train coming.
seize	A verb meaning 'to grab hold of something suddenly'. **Seize** him!

sew • so • sow

sew	A verb meaning 'to join with stitches'.
so	An adverb that has many meanings. Here are some: Do not walk **so** fast. Is that **so**? You are **so** kind.
sow	A verb meaning 'to spread seeds on the earth'.
sow	A noun (rhymes with 'cow')—a female pig.

shear • sheer

shear	A verb meaning 'to cut the hair or wool from an animal'. It is time to **shear** the sheep. The plural, shears, is a noun meaning 'the large clippers used to cut the wool'.
sheer	An adjective meaning 'very thin, so that you can see through'. **sheer** curtains It also means 'complete or absolute'. **sheer** luck It can mean 'very steep' as well. a **sheer** drop

side • sighed

side	A noun—the edges of an object; or a position. She touched the **side** of the car.

sighed	Past tense of the verb 'to sigh'. He **sighed** when he saw the long queue.

sight • site • cite

	See: cite • sight • site on p. 106.

some • sum

some	An adjective that does not tell exactly how many or how much. There are **some** apples in the basket.
sum	A noun meaning 'total'. The **sum** of 10 and 16 is 26.

son • sun

son	A noun meaning 'the male child of someone'.
Sun	A noun meaning 'the bright star that warms the Earth and lights the sky'.

stair • stare

stair	A noun meaning 'one of a number of steps'.
stare	A verb meaning 'to look at someone or something for a long time'.

stake • steak

stake	A noun—a stick with a point at one end.
steak	A noun—a thick piece of meat or fish for grilling or frying.

stalk • stork

stalk	A noun meaning 'the stem of a plant'; or a verb meaning 'to follow something very quietly'. The lion **stalks** its prey.
stork	A noun—a type of bird with long legs.

stationary • stationery

stationary	An adjective describing something that is still. The car was **stationary**.
stationery	A noun—writing paper and other writing material. I bought new **stationery** for school.

steal • steel

steal	A verb meaning 'to take something that does not belong to you'.
steel	A noun and an adjective to do with a type of metal made from iron. a **steel** helmet
steel	A verb meaning 'to harden'. **Steel** yourself; they're attacking.

storey • story

storey	A noun meaning 'one whole level of a building'.
story	A noun meaning 'a tale'. He told us an exciting **story**.

straight • strait

straight	An adjective meaning 'not bent or crooked'; 'honest' or 'serious'.
strait	A noun—a narrow channel joining two bodies of water. Bass **Strait** separates Tasmania from the rest of Australia.

tail • tale

tail	A noun meaning 'the end of the backbone of some animals'. The dog wagged its **tail**.
tale	A noun meaning 'a story'.

tear • tear

tear	A noun (rhymes with dear)—water produced by the eye.
tear	A noun (rhymes with bear)—a rip in something. Also a verb. a **tear** in his pants [noun] She could **tear** her dress if she climbed that fence. [verb]

their • there • they're

their	A possessive adjective used to show that something belongs to more than one person. **Their** noses are cold.
there	An adverb meaning 'in that place'. It is over **there**.
they're	The contraction of 'they are'. **They're** coming to see us.

theirs • there's

theirs	A possessive pronoun This project is **theirs**.
there's	The contraction of 'there is'. **There's** a cow in the front garden!

threw • through

threw	The past tense of the verb 'to throw'. Jenny **threw** the ball further than I.
through	Often a preposition beginning a phrase. The ship passed **through** the canal.

tied • tide

tied	The past tense and past participle of the verb 'to tie'. I **tied** the horse to the gate. [past tense] I have **tied** my shoelace with a double knot. [past participle]
tide	A noun meaning 'the rise and fall of the ocean'.

to • too • two

to	A preposition meaning 'towards'. Also part of the infinitive of verbs. Come **to** me. **to** eat, **to** sleep
too	An adverb meaning 'also'. It can also mean 'more than what is wanted'. He came, **too**. **too** fat
two	A noun and an adjective—the number 2. **two** brown cows [adjective]

toe • tow

toe	A noun—one of the five end parts of your foot.
tow	A verb meaning 'to drag something using a rope or chain'.

wail • whale

wail	A verb meaning 'to make a long, mournful cry'.
whale	A noun—a type of large mammal that lives in the sea.

waist • waste

waist	A noun—the middle part of your body, just above your hips.
waste	A verb meaning 'to use something in an extravagant way'. Don't **waste** water!
waste	A noun or an adjective to do with rubbish. They collect their **waste** in a bin. [noun] He is a **waste** collector. [adjective]

wait • weight

wait	A verb meaning 'to stay until something happens'. I **waited** at the bus stop.
weight	A noun—an amount of heaviness. What is the **weight** of this bag?

ware • wear • where

ware	A noun—goods that a merchant sells. It is often plural and often joined to other words, for example 'hardware'. There are lots of **wares** for sale at the market.
wear	A verb meaning 'to be dressed in something'. Did you **wear** your new suit?
where	An adverb or conjunction asking 'in what place'. **Where** did you get that funny hat?

way • weigh

way	A noun—how to do something; or the path you take. This is the **way** to the airport.
weigh	A verb meaning 'to find out how heavy a thing is'. **Weigh** yourself on the scales.

weak • week

weak	An adjective meaning 'not strong or powerful'. He is a very **weak** person.
week	A noun meaning 'a period of seven days'.

weather • whether

weather	A noun—sunshine, rain, cloud, wind or snow, etc.
whether	A conjunction meaning 'if it is the case that'. I asked **whether** he was going.

we'd • weed

we'd	Contraction of 'we would'. **We'd** better behave on the excursion.
weed	A noun—a nuisance plant. A **weed** came up in the middle of his potato patch.
weed	A verb—the act of removing weeds from the garden. I often help Dad **weed** the herb garden.

which • witch

which	A relative pronoun.

	Which would you like?
	We ate apples, **which** were delicious.
witch	A noun meaning 'a woman who carries out magic'.

who's • whose

who's	The contraction of 'who is'.
	Who's coming to the fair?
whose	A possessive pronoun or possessive adjective showing ownership.
	Whose book is this?

wind • wind

wind	A noun (rhymes with 'thinned')—moving air.
wind	A verb (rhymes with 'kind') meaning 'to change direction or twist around'.
	The road seemed to **wind** round the mountain.

wood • would

wood	A noun meaning 'the hard part of a tree'. Also means 'land covered by trees'.
	I walked through the **wood**.
would	An auxiliary verb
	I **would** like an apple.

wound • wound

wound	A noun (rhymes with 'tuned')—an injury.
wound	(Rhymes with 'hound'.) The past tense and past participle of the verb 'to wind'.
	He **wound** the fishing line onto the cork.

yore • your • you're

yore	A noun meaning 'a long time ago'.
	In days of **yore**, knights wore suits of armour.
your	A possessive adjective
	Your homework was very untidy.
you're	The contracted form of 'you are'.
	Are you sure **you're** coming to my birthday party?

Making sense

Errors to avoid

Absolute words

Some words are complete in themselves; they cannot be more or less.

Say: ✓ Everything is perfect.

Not: ✗ Everything is ~~more perfect~~.

Other absolute words include:

alive   correct   dead   final   unique

Agreement

Words in sentences must agree in person and number.

Say: ✓ The **captain** of the team will make **his** (or **her**) decision.

Not: ✗ The **captain** of the team will make ~~their~~ decision.

Say: ✓ **Each** child in the class **is** writing.

Not: ✗ **Each** child in the class ~~are~~ writing.

Dangling words and phrases (dangling modifiers)

Do not leave words or phrases dangling. That is, they must be correctly attached to their nouns, pronouns or verbs.

Say: ✓ While I was answering the telephone, the cat ate the fish.

Not: ✗ ~~While answering the telephone~~, the cat ate the fish.

The first sentence means that the cat ate the fish while the person who is speaking was answering the telephone. The second sentence means that the cat ate the fish while the cat was answering the telephone! (See Words in the wrong place, p. 124.)

Double negatives

A double negative is the use of two negatives in the same clause. The negatives cancel each other out. Double negatives are not acceptable in spoken or written form.

✗ I don't know nothing.

The negatives **don't** and **nothing** cancel each other out. This sentence actually means, *I know something.*

Matching lists or series

Make sure that lists or series match. Don't mix nouns with verbs in the same list.

Say: ✓ You can go by train, bus, car or plane.

Not: ✗ You can go by train, bus, car **or fly**.

Improving your writing

Clichés

Clichés (say *klee-shays*) are tired, overused words and phrases. Try to avoid them.

Here are some examples of clichés:

as old as the hills   as sick as a dog

Clichés can be used in conversation to give special effects, but always try to find fresh, new comparisons if you can.

Double meanings

Sometimes, the words we use can have more than one meaning. Always make sure that the words you use are clear and easy to understand.

eating apples	This phrase might mean apples that are good for eating, that someone is eating apples, or that the apples are eating.
beautiful girl's dress	This phrase might mean the dress of a beautiful girl or the beautiful dress of a girl.

(See Words with different meanings p. 124.)

Mixed metaphors or similes

When you use metaphors or similes as comparisons, be careful not to mix up ideas that don't go together.

For example, do not write:

They flew at each other like raging elephants.

This is a mixed simile, because elephants are not likely to fly!

A metaphor is a comparison that doesn't use the words *like* or *as*. It picks out some special feature that is common between two things.

Overused words

There are a number of words that writers tend to use too much. Try to find other words for words like *nice*, *fantastic*, *brilliant* and *great*. They are overused.

It is better to write: He is a very friendly (or pleasant) person.

than: He is a very nice person.

It is better to write: The movie was interesting (or fascinating).

than: The movie was fantastic.

Other overused words include:

awesome   fabulous   got   tremendous

You can leave out *got* on many occasions.

It is better to write: I have a red bike.

than: I have **got** a red bike.

Prepositions at the ends of sentences

Try not to use prepositions at the ends of sentences.

It is better to write: I fell **into** this water.

than: This is the water I fell **into**.

Sexist language

If you use words in ways that leave out males or females when they should be included, you are using sexist language. Sexist language should be avoided at all times.

It is better to write:

firefighter	than	fireman/firewoman
doctor	than	lady doctor
actor	than	actress
nurse	than	male nurse.

Slang

Slang is everyday, informal, spoken language that is not used in formal writing, except for special effect.

It is better to write: I feel sick.

than: I feel crook.

It is better to write: Throw me the ball.

than: Chuck me the ball.

Split infinitive

It is better in most cases to keep both parts of the infinitive together.

It is better to write: **to walk** quickly

than: **to** quickly **walk**.

The infinitive is the basic form of a verb. It has no subject, and is usually preceded by the word *to*.

Unnecessary words

Do not use words that mean the same thing as other words that you have already used.

It is better to write:

advance	than	advance forwards
descend	than	descend downwards
my autobiography	than	my own autobiography.

Vague words

Do not use vague words when you need to be precise.

a big dog

The dog may be tall or fat—or both! Say exactly what you mean.

Wordiness

Some people use too many words to say something. The rule is: be economical. Don't use two (or more) words where one will do!

It is better to write: now

than: at this point in time.

Words in the wrong place

Be careful where you place words in sentences.

The following sentence does not have a precise meaning because of the placement of the word *only*.

Tennis shoes **only** will be worn on the court.

This sentence suggests that players can wear nothing but tennis shoes!

In this case it would be better to rewrite the sentence with something like this:

Tennis shoes will be the **only** footwear permitted on this court.

This sentence makes it clear that the players must wear tennis shoes.

Words with different meanings

If words have more than one meaning, use them with care.

'Throw down your arms!' shouted the general.

Does the general want people to throw down their weapons, or a part of their bodies?

Figurative language

There are many ways that we can make our language colourful, rich and varied. Here just a few.

Alliteration

Alliteration is the repetition of the first sounds in words.

Pop the popcorn in the pot.

A ruby red rose

Imagery

Imagery is the use of vivid language to represent things and ideas. *Metaphors, similes* and *personification* are examples of imagery.

Simile

A simile is a direct comparison between things that uses the words **like** or **as**.

eyes that twinkled **like** stars

as quick **as** a flash

Metaphor

A metaphor is a comparison that doesn't use the words *like* or *as*. It picks out some special feature that is common between two things that are vastly different in every other way.

The road was **a ribbon of moonlight**.

The sea was **a sheet of unbroken glass**.

She is **a tiger on the football field**.

Personification

Personification means to give lifeless things the qualities of a living creature.

The trees bowed in the wind.

The sun smiled down on us.

Neologism

A neologism is a new word that has come into the language. Neologisms appear from many different sources, such as literature, science and technology.

cyberspace   internet   google

Nonsense verse

Nonsense verse is a light verse that relies on fanciful, invented words and phrases; humorous, impossible situations; and creative, witty language.

'Twas brillig, and the slithy toves

Did gyre and gimble in the wabe …'

From *Jabberwocky*, by Lewis Carroll

Many nursery rhymes are examples of nonsense verse.

Onomatopoeia

Onomatopoeia words are words that imitate or suggest the sounds they describe.

The wind **whistled.**

The leaves **rustled.**

The brakes **screeched.**

Animal noises are a good source of onomatopoeic words.

meow	oink	chirp
growl	baa	woof

Rhyme

Rhyme is the repetition of the same or similar sounds in words. It is common in poems, usually at the ends of lines.

Ten Red Petals

Ten red petals on the **rose**,

One mosquito on my **nose**.

Ten brown speckles on the **egg**,

Two mosquitoes on my **leg**.

Ten strong sailors on the **deck**,

Three mosquitoes on my **neck**.

SPLAT!

Rhythm

A rhythm is any recurring beat. It is important in literature. There are many different types of rhythm in poetry.

Read the following poem slowly, and listen to the rhythm:

It's Raining

Drip drip drop

Splish splash splop

Dribble dribble

Gurgle gurgle

Slop slop slop

Word play

Word play is a literary technique that plays with words to create an amusing or witty effect. Two common forms of word play are the pun and spoonerism.

- Pun

  The pun relies on the fact that some words or phrases have two meanings.

  I wondered why the football was getting bigger. Then it hit me.

  I'm reading a book about anti-gravity. It's impossible to put down.

  When a clock is hungry it goes back four seconds.

- Spoonerism

  A spoonerism is a deliberate error in speech, made by switching sounds or parts of words around for humorous effect.

  flutter by ➜ butterfly

  Tease my ears. ➜ Ease my tears.

  I hit my bunny phone. ➜ I hit my funny bone.

The affix

Affixes are word parts (also known as *morphemes)* that are attached to the beginning or end of a *root word* (also known as a *base word*) and change its meaning.

There are two types of affix: *prefix* and *suffix*.

Prefixes

A prefix is attached to the beginning of a root word.

Here are some common prefixes:

Prefix	Meaning	Example
anti-	against, opposed to	antiwar, antibiotic
bi-	two	bicycle, biannual
co-	together	cooperate, co-author
milli-	one thousand	milligram, millimetre
non-	not	nonexistent, nonprofitable
post-	after	postwar, postscript
pre-	before	preheat, prehistoric
re-	back, again	return, replay
semi-	half	semicircle, semicolon
un-	not	unable, unaffected
sub-	under	submarine, submerge

Suffixes

A suffix is attached to the end of a root word.

Here are some common suffixes:

Suffix	Meaning	Example
-al	forms a noun from a verb	refusal, betrayal
-dom	state of, forms a noun	freedom, kingdom
-en	forms verbs, adjectives and plurals	strengthen, woollen, children
-ful	full of, forms adjectives	plateful, joyful
-ic	forms adjectives	volcanic, angelic
-ism	forms nouns	heroism
-ist	one who practises something, forms nouns	geologist, pharmacist
-less	without something, forms adjectives	harmless, sugarless
-like	has the characteristic of, forms adjectives	childlike, catlike
-ly	forms adverbs from adjectives	quickly, solidly

Origins of words

Modern English has many sources. It has borrowed from many other languages. It is a living language, so it continues to change. New words are added, some are dropped and some change their meanings.

Knowing the origins of words and their parts helps us read, write and understand our language better.

Here are some examples of word origins:

Word	Original language	Origin
autograph	Greek	*autos*: self *graphein*: to write
brother	Old English	*brothor*: brother
curry	Tamil	*kari*: curry
easel	Dutch	*exel*: easel
egg	Old Norse	*eggja*: egg
vitamin	Latin	*vita*: life

index